Barge Farm
B.M.73.7
Path
Headpile Ait
Amerden House
B.M.72.7
Def.
Sur. 77·7
Albion P.H.
Iron Fou
Disused
Bray
B.M.78.2
Bray Mead
Arbour Lane
Monkey Hall Hotel
B.M.74.3
The Hut
Lodge
The Cut
B.M.70.0
B.M.88.5
B.M.78.7
B.M.69.7
Well
Spring

To Anne & Ron.
for you New House.
January 1976

BRAY
TODAY
&
YESTERDAY

Village from Church Tower, 1972

BRAY TODAY & YESTERDAY

NAN BIRNEY

Thames Valley Press
Maidenhead and Trowbridge
1973

This edition first Published by
Thames Valley Press, Maidenhead 1973

ISBN 0 90029 414 O

Photoset and printed
by Redwood Press Limited
Trowbridge, Wiltshire

Dedication

In 1970 a pamphlet issued by the Bray Preservation Society was delivered to every house. It was headed "This is Your Village", and asked for opinions on the future existence and development of Bray.

It was a singularly apt statement, emphasize whichever word you will, for Bray is like that – it draws people and holds them. It has warmth and humour. Few have left voluntarily or without a backward look.

So, I ask you to join me in a toast—

"To Bray! This is our village."

Preface

In setting out to record and research the history of the houses of Bray I have found that libraries tend to have but two sub-headings. "Bray. Vicar of" and "Bray. Hundred of", but patient perseverance can uncover from Berkshire County records various references to Bray. Inevitably the later refer to earlier authors, with but few additions of their own. Thus it seemed that were I to quote all of them it would produce a larger book than planned. Also it would be on a par with the, doubtless apocryphal, remark of the uneducated foreigner whose comment on a performance of "Hamlet" was that he "didn't think much of it – it was full of quotations." Nevertheless it has become obvious that a historian could produce a fuller account than this. Let us hope that somebody, some day, will do so.

I have endeavoured to sketch in, in broad strokes, the earlier history, in an attempt to provide a backcloth to the developments up to the period which is vouched for by personal memories. These last are the facts, so far unrecorded, which may be of use to future researchers and I hope may interest readers today and form a small addition to the sparse literature on the subject.

It is probably inevitable that there are omissions and errors – I invite any substantiated corrections and additions which could be of value in any subsequent writing.

The area dealt with here is limited to Bray Village, Canon Hill, Braywick, east of the A.308, and the Monkey Island area. A limited acreage, but it forms the bulk of what is loosely termed Bray at this time.

I am indebted to the Ordnance Survey Department for permission to print, in advance of publication in 1974, the relevant part of the new map of Bray, though with the rapid increase in housing, this map, prepared in 1972, will inevitably be incorrect by the time it reaches the general public.

Signposts to research and help with facts have been provided by Rev. S.W. Doran; a previous Clerk to the Bray

Parish Council; Captain Turk, Swan-master to Her Majesty Queen Elizabeth II; the Jones family, who gave generously of their time and knowledge as did also several "senior citizens" born and bred here, who have added flesh to the bones of 20th century statistics; officers of Cookham R.D.C. and Bray Parish Council; also some residents who have helped by discovering at least some of the past history of their homes.

It has been somewhat of a jig-saw puzzle to fit the many and various pieces of information into their proper places. But it can be said to have been a co-operative effort in which memories, files, archives, and family photograph albums have been searched for appropriate materials.

To all who have contributed I say a heartfelt, "Thank you."

Berkeleys, N. Birney
Vicarage Lane, April 1973
Bray

Contents

Plates

Photographs 1972/3 – Ian Bloomfield

Text Illustrations

PART ONE

DAWN TO DOMESDAY-PLUS

Once upon a time Bray was not.

That is to say, it had no name.

Land there was, water there was, trees a-many and wilde beastes among them. Archaeologists have discovered, in the past 5 years, that even in the mezolithic period there were human habitations too, though it is not possible to estimate how many, now that most of the land is built-up. Water being the pre-requisite of living, the river and streams provide the most fruitful source for investigation, and the Bray reach has yielded many objects. Among them are a neo lithic antler and chisel-edged implements; a bronze axe, spear-head and flints. A mammoth's tusk and bones of ox, pig, sheep, deer, horse, and goat bear witness to man's furred friends or enemies. A comb made from a deer's antler is thought to have been for use on hides rather than human hair and dates from neolithic times.

While some very early settlement may have existed it is unlikely to have been at our village level where it was so densely wooded and damp. Man may have followed the river on his way to the higher land at Taplow and beyond, perhaps stopping for a fish-dinner en route, but it is not until the letters A.D. appear in records that any indication is found of settlements at Thames-level.

When there was any reason to travel westwards the route chosen would be on higher, drier land. It is therefore probable that the first well worn, and subsequently strengthened track followed, roughly, the line of the present A.308.

There is evidence that the Romans passed this way, for Roman coins, weapons, and fragments of armour were found at the close of the 18th century "in East-hay, a common field to the east of Bray" and a short length of Roman highway "between the river and the east end of the churchyard." At Braywick a Roman road led north to Cockmarsh, Cookham, and at Cox Green there was a Romano-British villa probably in use 150–350 A.D. An attractive painting portraying its probable appearance is in the Reitlinger Museum in Maidenhead. Roman coins were also found in a garden of the Hibbert Road cottages. Braywick may well have been a Roman halting-place, deriving its name from the Roman Vicus, a village (and retained by the Saxons as Wica, a farm) and offering some means of refreshment to the tough and efficient road-builders.

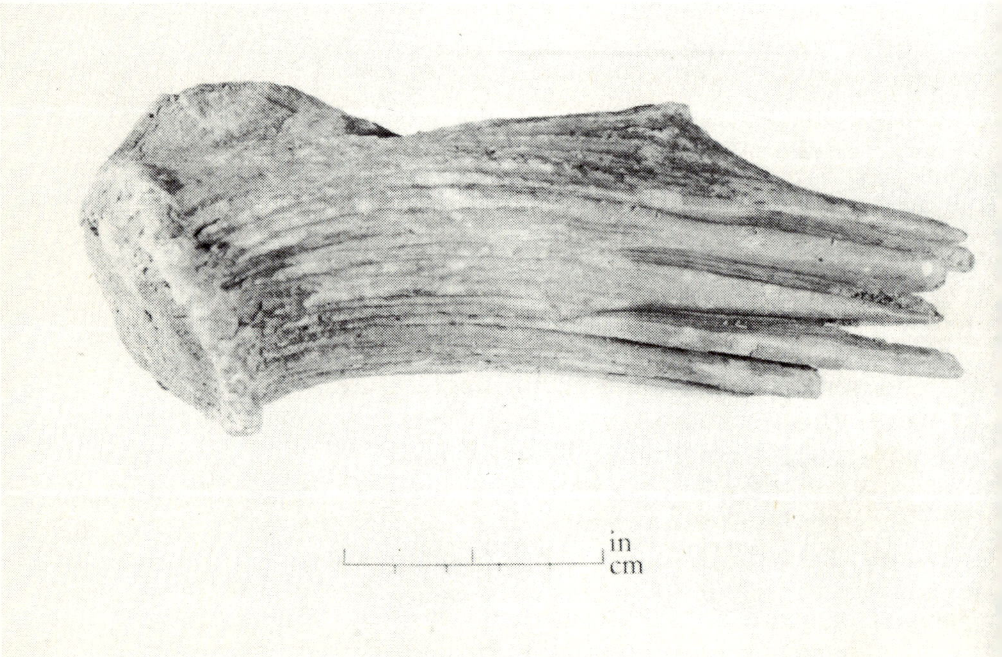

Antler Comb

Excavations from 1969–72 behind Bray Marina discovered a number of skeletons, one of which is of an unusually tall woman of about 350 A.D. These, together with implements for metal-working of the same period, and probable jetty into the river lead to the theory that there was a settlement and burial-ground near by.

If this is so they may well have trodden-out a lesser road beside the river to reach the ford at the bottom of Ferry Road. Here the water ran shallow in early times, providing a useful crossing not only for farmers and hunters but also for any would-be travellers to Taplow. There is one memory today of such a route being known, in her childhood (1880–90) as "the Roman walk."

With an increase in the number of settlements roads joining them would have been needed, and it is probable they would have run like ribs from the higher spines as well as following the course of the rivers. So, we have Braywick linked to Bray; and the Upper Bray Rd, which was called Holyport Road until a few years ago. The lower Bray Rd to Maidenhead is thought to have arrived much later.

The Saxons probably found our village to their liking for, in the parish accounts and elsewhere it is differentiated from the other areas (Tutchens, Ffifield, Monyrewe, Okeley, and Braywick) as being Bray Town. Since "town" is derived from the Saxon "ton" meaning "a forest clearing containing a farm," it may have been just that, and for centuries the name stuck. There is evidence too in the recovery of the prow of a Viking ship during the excavation for Bray Marina (now in Reading Museum).

Cooper King wrote that "Bray ceased to be important when the Roman lines of communication, which had created it, were abandoned." Nationally, maybe – but there was reported to be a Saxon church here, so there must have been at least a small population to use it. There are no contemporary records, but we can probably picture Bray Town as having a mill (still standing); farms to supply it; a tannery for treating the hides of animals hunted in Windsor

Forest, and a wharf for receiving their delivery by water. Whether "The Tan House" is on this site we know not but many animals' skulls and bones have been dug up recently from its garden. Certainly in 1637 there is recorded a "Tann-Howse by the river". The location is not specified except that it was between Maidenhead and Windsor. Enquiries in Windsor have failed to provide any claim by them to having had a tannery, so until further notice I claim this one for Bray!

At this time the country was organised into juridical and named areas. Shires were divided into thirds, or trythings. Each trything into Hundreds, or wapentakes (a wapentake referred to the system of voting by raising weapons – or wapens). Each Hundred was based on the representation of 100 families, which would, of course, have been the lords of the manor, and land-owners. Bray was one of the "Seven Hundreds of Cookham and Bray" and the "Court of the Seven Hundreds" was at Braywick.

The hundred families would have had employees for the various farm and household activities, housed in cottages. Most of the manors would also be expected to provide fighting-men for the king, but in the case of Bray this was waived, "as Brai lay in the Furest (i.e. Windsor Forest)" and could be commanded only by the king.

Domesday Survey. When, why, and how came the name Bray? There are three theories.

The earliest, chronologically, is pre-Domesday Survey and is supported by the Oxford Dictionary of English place-names, quoted to me by Mr. G. White of Old Mill Lane; also by Mr. Michael Bayley A.R.I.B.A. This takes the origin back to the Old English BRĒG, meaning a brow, or the brow of a hill. The idea is that the high land from the Thicket southwards, and curving to take in Canon Hill, would form the brow. An additional point of Mr. White's is that if the settlement had the name Bray at the time of the Domesday Book it is hardly likely to have come from

France.

The next two theories are related by, among others, Kerry. He quotes one possibility of its being related to Bibracte, an early tribe inhabiting the northern part of "the hundred."

Lastly, his own choice which links it with the French, . . . "derived from BRAIUM, which in the ancient language of the Gauls, signifies 'Puddle,' 'Marsh,' or 'Moist place.' " And he goes on to to give examples of French place names incorporating Bray, or brai, "all of which places have taken their names from the wet and marshy nature of the ground on which they are situated."

The Domesday Survey map of BERROCHESCIRE (Berks) shows BRAI as a large area with bounds from Maidenhead Bridge to the Thicket; southwards to Touchen End; east to Oakley Green and The Willows; and thence north via the river to the bridge. This formed the Hundred. Within it was a "vill" in which were "King's manors and holdings" also named BRAI.

The evidence for the Bibracte theory is scant and unreliable. The BREG appears a possibility. But my own choice is for the French "moist place."

In aiming at the high points one would have been only too aware of the unpleasant traversing of the damp, oppressive lands. Who could have blamed those early cartographers had they added angrily to their maps "Heere bee bogges"? They may have heard local people speak of BRĒG, agreed whole-heartedly with their diagnosis as they heard it spoken but spelled it in their own way, BRAI.

The written record states:-

"The King (William I) holds BRAI in demesne. King Edward held it. There are 18 hides and they did not pay geld. On the demesne there are 3 ploughs and there are 5 villeins and 7 bordars with 25 ploughs. There are 4 serfs and a church and 3 knights (milites) and 50 acres of meadows, and woodland to render 60 swine. Reimbald holds one hide which belongs to the church and there he has one plough."

It may be of interest here to explain some of the terms used in the above paragraph.

Demesne – Domain, is landed property.

Geld – The Crown tax paid under Anglo-Saxon and Norman Kings.

Hide and plough are of roughly equivalent value in being 100–120 acres. "As much as would support one free family and dependants." It would necessitate the keeping of eight oxen or horses to work it.

Villein – a tenant who held his land (usually a virgate, or 30 acres) in return for menial services to his lord.

Bordar – a feudal tenant holding a cottage and a few acres, and bound to menial service.

Serfs were virtually slaves, for they were servants on the land, and in any change of property-ownership they were transferred with it, willy-nilly.

Milites would be pledged to military service whenever necessary, but the records imply that Bray was reckoned to be of more value "Digging for Victory" than fighting for it!

So, rural life continued.

In Henry III's reign there were ploughmen, shepherds, and swineherds, each of whom held half a virgate and were found herbage or pasture for their own beasts. At shearing time they were given the "wombeslokes" (the edges of the fleece). They formed a body of additional part-time labour for the manor.

Their wages, in 1254, were:-

Shepherd and carters	5 shillings p.a.
Dairymen	4s 6d p.a.
Plough drivers	5 shillings p.a.
Plough holders	12s 9d p.a.

And all had an allowance of corn from the harvest.

Boats were then plying on the river, too. The charge at Bray wharf being 4d for each load.

Though the manor of Bray belonged to the King it was usually assigned to the Queen (until Edward VI's time, when he gave it to the Bishop of Oxford).

In 1293 the churchwardens appealed to Queen Margaret to persuade the parishioners to pay their shares for rebuilding the church. She sent her Beadle of the Manor to collect the money from an unwilling populace. The then Vicar, Roger, must have been grateful for the Royal assistance, having, presumably, failed to convince the landlords of their duties.

(Would there were such a Beadle today to help the Church Finance Committee find the means of repair and upkeep of today's building! "*Plus ça change . . .*")

For some three centuries Bray and Braywick continued with only local difficulties.

The law, administered at the Manor Court (in Hibbert Rd, later Braywick School) dealt with offenders of all sorts, including one woman with a wicked tongue (garulatrix). The nearest stocks and whipping-post were at Touchen End, but it seems that fines or a spell in a cell were more usual discouragements.

Stewards, bailiffs and seneschals watched over the welfare and success of the Hundreds.

While the Kings and their armies marched and fought over most of Berkshire, Bray had no great sufferings and one may guess that they pursued their forestry, farming, fishing, and tanning without undue pressures. New buildings during these years included the church; Lychgate and St. Michael's Cottage; Vicarage Cottage; Stuart Cottage and Shottery for foresters; the Crown Inn, at first 2 cottages; and the Chauntry of the Virgin, which appears on all maps with the appended date 1330, though it may well have been earlier. There may also have been a "poorhouse" on the site of today's Chauntry House, and its gardener's cottage across the road is of early date.

There is no record of a vicarage, but some suggest the priest may have lived over the Lychgate.

Among the agricultural workers conditions changed considerably. Serfdom disappeared, and there was a continuous progress towards regimes more akin to today's.

Came Henry VIII and his quarrel with Rome. The only outward and visible change in Bray was the closing of the Chauntry Chapel and the departure of its priest. The Vicar, Simon Aleyn managed to stay with his flock by dint of acquiescing to his Sovereign, both then and subsequently, as occasion demanded.

He was not the only cleric to be so accommodating, but he was the only one to achieve recognition for generations to come by having his exploits set to words and music, even though it was historically inaccurate.

Charles II seems to have made some impression locally. Maybe his visit to Nell Gwynne at Philibert's included some digression to Braywick and Bray Town before returning to Windsor?

During his reign the Great Plague took its toll. There are rumours that bodies were brought by river to Bray and buried in the present Vicarage garden, and behind the Old Schoolroom. The latter is proved wrong by the dating of the skull I found (among many other bones in the same place) as being Saxon. By the end of the reign Bray had its first school "for poor boys" at the Old Schoolroom (1682); there were a few new cottages; the Vicarage is now known to have been by the river in 1677. Most of the bread-winners still served the estates and larger houses but there were the beginnings of "private enterprise" in the form of merchants and craftsmen.

Jesus Hospital had been caring for the elderly since 1628 and Rixmans Charity is providing for the clothing and apprenticing of two poor boys every three years, also £2 per annum to "two of the godliest poor" is given under Dr. Challoner's Gift, though it had to be shared with two others from East Okley. Presumably 10s (or 50p today) was a real help in those days.

The 18th century saw the advent of a few houses, rather than small cottages, in the villages. Monkey Island, The Limes, Rickhams, Chauntry House, were among them,

Lady Coleraine was in Canon Hill House, and gave Bray a fire-engine. The village's first shop opened – Mr. Jones', in the High Street, where it has remained for two centuries.

The "gentry" and "employees" attitude was to persist here as elsewhere for a further hundred years, but "traders" were being differentiated from farmers and farm labourers, and developments towards the main period of the rest of this book were progressing.

So, let us see the houses extant today, and how and when they were added to the scene.

PART TWO

LETS GO WALKABOUT

PARISH CHURCH OF ST MICHAEL, BRAY

Among all the houses of Bray described in this book, the House of God, the parish church of St. Michael, is the most ancient and historic. The present building dates from 1293, and was planned on a lavish scale for a village church, for it consists of a chancel 43 ft. by 15 ft., a nave and north and south aisles each 85 ft. by 16 ft. 9 in., which gives a sense of great spaciousness to the body of the church, a tower at the south-west of the south aisle 15 ft. square internally, north and south chapels 28 ft. by 17 ft. 4 in., a north vestry, and a detached Lady Chapel on the north side of the churchyard.

Throughout the centuries the church has been altered and restored in various ways, but it suffered a series of sweeping 'restorations' in the Victorian era. In 1859 the gallery at the west end of the nave was removed. The north arcade of the chancel, the eastern arch of which was widened early in the 16th century, was rebuilt to match the south arcade, while the east window of the Chapel of St. Nicholas, on the north, was altered from five lights to four and the two north windows from four lights to two. An organ was obtained and adapted to fit between the windows on the north wall. The Chapel of All Saints on the south side was given an 'early perpendicular' character, and the 13th century chancel arch was reconstructed.

The Vicar of the time, the Reverend Austen Leigh, nephew of Jane Austen, has recorded: "At the junction of the nave with the chancel there was, on each side, a thick mass of old wall extending both across the nave and also laterally westward between the nave and each aisle, so that the voice of the officiating minister would scarcely be heard in the eastern parts of the church. The chancel arch itself was low and narrow, so that the east window could scarcely be seen from the west end of the church." The work of reconstruction was entrusted to T. Wyatt, and was intended to provide "a wider, higher and more ornamental chancel arch, opening to view the whole length of the church from west to east." Those portions of the old walls which projected westward on each side of the chancel arch were cut away, and two wider arches were constructed to embrace the wider space thus thrown open. That on the north side was built of stone; that on the south side was formed of the old chalk from the 13th century arches which were destroyed. Arches were also provided to divide the north and south chapels from the aisles, making five new arches.

Bray Churchyard

By 1862 the work of 'restoration' was in full flood. The north wall was entirely rebuilt; but the windows were replaced precisely as they had been before, and Mr. Wyatt even preserved an angular projection which had marked the stair case to the rood loft. The walls of the nave were raised about six feet, clerestory windows were added, and the nave and aisles were reroofed. Eight new pillars were inserted in the nave arcade, replacing the old pillars of chalk which were much decayed and broken. The nave and aisles were then reseated with the pews which are in use today. The church had been repewed in 1840, in a rather unusual manner: "Along the aisles were ranged four tiers of pews, each tier being raised higher than the tier in front of it, so that the occupants of the two aisles looked toward each other across the church. The seats in the nave extended across the nave, without any passage up the centre." In this operation of 1840 the monumental stones were removed from their proper positions and arranged as pavement without any regard to the graves to which they belonged. The last burial permitted within the walls of the church took place in 1853. The reseating of 1862 in the new 'open plan' church meant that nave, aisles and chapels were filled with pews. The organ had already been placed in the St. Nicholas' Chapel, and the font which had been under the reading desk near the chancel arch was moved to the All Saints' Chapel.

The plan of an English medieval parish church, such as we have at Bray, is the result of an attempt to combine into one whole a series of compartments, and the most typical feature is the long chancel. It is important to remember that the long chancels of medieval England were built to provide a place where the parochial clergy and those attached to the chantry altars of a church could say their offices together. They were only occasionally used by the laity, and they were not intended to provide a place for a choir of lay singers. Today some people delight in the unbroken vistas to be found in many of our cathedrals and parish churches, and the sight of a high altar from the back of a long church, as did Mr. Austen Leigh. This is something quite alien to the medieval mind. The Victorian principles of arranging a church had their unhappiest results when applied to medieval buildings. At Bray the chancel was furnished with a double row of choir stalls on each side, although a surpliced choir was not introduced until 1875, steps were inserted at the east end of the sanctuary in order that the altar could be seen beyond the chancel furnishings. The whole church thus became one place of worship, with only one altar.

This did not last for long. One of Mr. Austen Leigh's successors decided to re-establish the Chapel of All Saints. The font was moved to its present position at the west end of the south aisle, an altar was placed under the east window, and the pews which were facing across the church were turned to face east. This area was no longer an extension of the chancel and associated with the choir, and for Sunday services the congregation was forced back to the south aisle. On the north side, the congregational pews were cleared away and a new and much larger organ provided, the congregation retreating to the north aisle. Thus the choir was left literally 'out on a limb' with the high altar far from the people, and on great festivals only about one-third of the people in the church could even see the celebrant, and even less could hear him until a voice reinforcement system was introduced in 1960.

These difficulties are in varying measure common to all medieval churches which have passed through a Victorian restoration, and succeeding generations have grappled with the problem of re-arranging churches so that the liturgy can be offered in a simpler, more direct, and corporate way, and yet preserve all that is best in the Victorian tradition, with its emphasis on the altar as something which must be visible from every part of the church and on the church itself, expressing the mystery and splendour of Christian worship. There is today a new sense of the meaning of the Church as the people of God and the Body of Christ. A deepened understanding of the Holy Communion and of its social implications, and a growing recognition of the scandal of a divided Church have been further factors in the creation of a fresh outlook among Christians of many different traditions and loyalties.

These ideas lie behind the re-arrangement of the church which was made in 1968. No alterations were made to the fabric of the building, but a new sanctuary area was formed within the first bay of the nave, with a free-standing altar and identical balancing ambos. The organ was moved from the north chapel and rebuilt at the west end of the north aisle over the choir vestry, and the Chapel of St. Nicolas was then refurnished. The choir was moved to the east end of the north aisle facing across the new sanctuary, taking advantage of the enlarged arches of the nave arcade altered in 1862. While this work was in process, a discarded chancel screen from Cookham was acquired and adapted for use across the south aisle to screen the Chapel of All Saints, and on this screen was placed the Royal Arms of James I, removed from the old chancel screen when it was destroyed in the Victorian restoration.

The parish church today is thus being used again in a manner which would surely have been approved by the medieval builders. The nave and aisles with the new sanctuary are used for the Sunday services and for large services; the chancel is used for the daily offices every weekday; the chapels are used for weekday Communion services and for the services of Guilds and organisations connected with the Church.

Brass rubbing is now so popular that a brief note of the brasses at Bray must be given. On the north wall of the north aisle is the brass of Sir John de Foxley (d. 1378), containing the figure of a knight in bascinet with camail, and plates, standing between his two wives under a canopy now lost. The knight's head rests on a helm crested with a fox; his jupon is charged with his two bars. The lady on his right wears an armorial dress charged with Foxley impaling Brocas. The lady on his left is similarly dressed; her dress is charged with Foxley only. The figures and the canopy occupy the upper half of the slab; below is a fox, on which rests a column supporting the design. All inscriptions have disappeared. In the floor at the west end of the north aisle is a brass to Thomas Lawrence, who died 28th October 1603.

On the south wall of the south aisle, east of the south door, is a brass to William Dyer, Vicar of Bray 1396-1440. Beneath is a brass inscribed in black letters to Thomas atte Lude, chaplain. He was chaplain of the Chantry Chapel of St. Mary in the churchyard. In the west wall, south of the west door, is a brass with inscription to William Laken, a justice of the King's Bench, who died 6th October 1475, and his wife Sibyl, a daughter and heir of John Sifrewast, lord of Clewer. He wears a sword and belt and a long furred gown.

In the floor of the south aisle is a brass to William Smythe and his two wives Agnes and Matilda, c. 1490, with an inscription in black letters, a blank being left for the date. The chapel of All Saints, at the end of the south aisle, contains on the south wall a brass to Clement Kelke, haberdasher of London and merchant adventurer, who died in 1593, and his wife Elizabeth, daughter of Alderman Becher. On the same wall is a brass to William Smithe, 1594, gentleman-at-arms to Queen Mary and Queen Elizabeth. Above are his arms, viz: Sable a ring argent within a border engrailed or and a chief or with mace sable therein. The crest is a fore-arm cut off at the elbow, the hand grasping a mace. On the north side of the chapel, in the south-east pier of the nave, is a brass tablet in a marble frame, without name or date. It shows a man and a woman of c. 1600 kneeling in prayer. Below is an inscription beginning:-

'When Oxford gave thee two degrees in art,
And love possest thee master of my heart
Thy colledge fellowshipp thow lefs't for mine
And nought but death could seprate me fro thine.

Thirty-five years we lived in wedlocke bands
Conioyned in our hearts as well as handes
But death the bodies of best friends divides
And in the earth's close womb their relyckes hides
Yet here they are not lost but sowen, that they
May rise more glorious at the Judgment day.'

Two shields in the spandrel of the frame have apparently been repainted.

On the north face of the north-east pier of the nave is a brass to Arthur Page of Water Oakley, who died 23rd December 1610, and his wife Cicely, daughter of William Brownesopp, by whom he had issue one son, Edward; she died 12th March 1598. He is represented kneeling in prayer with his wife.

Among the many monuments in the church, two are of special interest. On the north wall of the chancel is a monument to William Goddard of Philibert, who died 1609, founder of Jesus Hospital, and Joyce Maunsell his wife, who died in 1622. Within two niches under an entablature and broken pediment supported by marble Corinthian columns are painted three-quarter figures, life-sized, of William Goddard and his wife. The inscriptions are on the base of the monument, which is of marble and painted stone. Over the entablature is a shield of arms: Gules an eagle or and a chief vair. William Goddard founded Jesus Hospital for forty poor people, and made the Wardens and the Commonalty of the Mystery of Fishmongers governors of the hospital for ever.

On the north wall of the north aisle is the monument of William Norreys, usher of the Parliament house and of the Order of the Garter under Mary and Elizabeth, who died 16th April 1591. He wears the badge of the Garter and kneels with his wife and twelve children. Above are his own arms and those of Fortescue for his wife, and between himself and his wife is the Norreys shield with the Motto 'Faithfully Sarve'. Below is Norreys impaling Fortescue.

Bray Church is said to have a treasury of Victorian glass.

The earliest work is the east window of the chancel, designed by G. E. Street and executed by Weales of Newcastle. It was given in 1856 by Mr. Hibbert in memory of his father, and the design included the ten last scenes from the life of our Lord. The Reverend George Welford, who had been a curate of Bray and chaplain of Jesus Hospital for more than twenty years, seeing that the central place contained a picture of the Crucifixion, expressed his fears that this might have a 'Romanising tendency'. Mr. Hibbert very patiently explained to him that in such a series the principal event could not well be omitted. Mr Welford was satisfied that no wrong was intended, and finally wrote and published a series of ten sermons on the ten different subjects of the window, and a copy of his work is preserved in the vestry.

In March 1860 the west window of the north aisle was reconstructed and filled with stained glass designed and executed by O'Connor in memory of Philip Coney. In May 1860 the west window of the nave was reconstructed and filled with stained glass to the designs of G. E. Street, and in September 1861 the west window of the south aisle was rebuilt and filled with stained glass as a memorial to the former Vicar, the Reverend Walter Levett. Mr. Wyatt was the architect, and the glass was executed by Hughes and Ward of Soho. Mr. Wyatt was also responsible for the reconstruction of the Chapel of All Saints, where the windows were executed by Lavers and Barraud. The same firm was responsible for the windows in the Chapel of St. Nicholas. By degrees all the windows were filled with stained glass, the gifts of various parishioners. The Royal Arms, now above the screen of the Chapel of All Saints, are unusual in that they are the arms of James I, carved for Bray Church in 1604. The Royal Arms in most old churches are those of Charles II; but at Bray at the time of the Commonwealth, the Royal Arms were hidden away and carefully guarded. In 1654 Commonwealth Arms were set up on the Rood screen at a cost of £1. 4. 0, and at the

Restoration these arms were burnt and the Royal Arms replaced. They remained above the Rood screen, described as of oak and handsomely carved, until the restoration of 1862 when they were placed on the wall above the south-west door. There they remained until the alterations of 1968 when they were again replaced on a screen and their beauty and carving on both sides could be seen.

The font and its cover dates from 1647. The silver Communion vessels of Bray, dating from 1638, were sold by the Vicar and Churchwardens in 1854 and replaced with vessels of much lighter weight. The parish has six chalices and patens and four flagons, some of little practical use in these days; but they are displayed on the high altar on great festivals, together with other silver items, in accordance with the old English custom. A black-letter copy of Foxe's 'Book of Martyrs' was formerly chained to a desk at the west end of the church. The book, with the chain attached to the cover is still preserved in the vestry, though in a very tattered condition; the greater portion of its contents having been filched by unscrupulous visitors. There is also a fine model in a glass case of Bray Church in 1850.

There is in the tower a peal of eight bells, the treble inscribed 'Feare God Honour the King 1678', the second by Henry Knight, 1612, the third by Henry Knight, 1613, the fourth by Thomas Mears, 1812, the fifth by Thomas Swain, 1771, while the tenor bears the date 1163, the seventh and eighth bells were added in 1948. Bray is still served by a devoted band of ringers, and Sunday by Sunday the bells ring out to call men and women to the activity for which this ancient building was erected and for which it still exists – the praise and worship of Almighty God.

Written for this book by Reverend Sidney W. Doran Instituted 1958.

VICARAGES, OLD AND NEW

Searches and researches failed to produce any firm statement as to the early accommodation for the Vicar – "Don't know" – "Have no records" – "It is thought that . . ." have come from the Church Commissioners, county archivists and historians. Even Kerry had to rely on local memories, saying that it "is reported to have been situated in a meadow on the south side of the church," but giving no real evidence.

Then, at the annual Church bazaar in 1972, Mr. Doran called to me across the hubbub, "Mrs. Birney! Old vicarage – Try the Diocesan Record Office at Salisbury," and gave me the address, adding ". . . and the best of British luck!"

"Ah, well," I thought, "nothing ventured . . .". My enquiry was promptly and helpfully answered. Six Bray terriers (records of sites and boundaries) existed, one of which gave the location of the Vicarage then already in existence, and obviously between church and river – its date – 1677.

> A terrier of all the glebe lands and tenements belonging to the Vickaridg of the parish of Bray in the Countey of Berks. Together with all thoas tithes which doe appertaine to the same. Made on the 30th of December in the year of our Lord God 1677. By the Vicker and Churchwardens of the said parish whose name are heerunto subscribed.
>
> Imprimis theire is a vickaridg house with a hale, Parlor and kitchin, Together with one studie and three Lodging Chambers with som other small roomes. Together with one barne and one smale stable with one orchard and garden and yard Conteining by estimations one acre of Lands be it more or lese, cituate lying or adioyning unto the river of Thames one the north part and one the south part one the Churchyard and one the west part one a ground theire Called garston and one the east part one a lane leading from Bray towne to the thames side.

This makes much more sense architecturally but makes one wonder why Kerry's account, in 1861, went unchallenged by the then Vicar, Rev. Austen Leigh, who surely must have known more about his own home.

Anyway, there we are – 1677 it was in being. How much earlier, and if so, when? To any further researchers I echo our Vicar's wishes ". . . the best of British luck!"

Now to look at the present and the past buildings.

ST. MICHAELS VICARAGE

This house was built in 1956 on land which used to be the kitchen-garden of the previous vicarage.

When Rev. Austen Leigh was vicar, in 1853, there used to be a public pathway through it from the churchyard to the bank of the river, and thence to Charlese (the present Waterside Inn) – he found this a nuisance, and so closed it, constructing in its stead the present pathway to Ferry Rd.

In 1954 the Church Commissioners at last realized that the 33-roomed vicarage was an unnecessary cross to lay on the shoulders of a modern incumbent. Retaining the kitchen-garden, they sold the remaining land, house and outbuildings to Mr. Victor Benjamin, of London, and built a smaller, modern vicarage. Originally it had 3 reception rooms, including a very small study, and 4 bedrooms, but Rev. Doran added a dining-room with a study above it, and bay windows to the small study and sitting room. Its garden is large by today's standards, but a 12 ft width of land on the South side was sold to Mr. Barton in 1971, enabling him to build his house adjoining the Vicarage land.

ST. MICHAELS HOUSE was built in 1963 on land owned by the

Church and previously occupied by a large barn.

Permanent accommodation was needed for Curates in a parish whose population was increasing, because of new building, at a prodigious rate.

A good brick building was erected, comprising a study, living-cum-dining room, and large kitchen on the ground floor. Above are three good bedrooms.

TUDOR HOUSE AND BERKELEYS

These two houses were formed in 1955 from one large building, the previous vicarage containing 33 rooms. Mr. Benjamin's architect knocked out the central portion, leaving Tudor House, (which is recorded in the archives at Salisbury as having been in existence in 1677) and Berkeley's which was built on after 1853 by Rev. Austen Leigh who had an ever-increasing family to accommodate. Today,

TUDOR HOUSE has a study; dining and sitting rooms; kitchen and cloakroom; 4 bedrooms and bathroom.

There are old beams in the dining-room, on the stairs and in one bedroom. The outhouses are unchanged from the time of Rev. Austen Leigh.

On the riverbank, in its garden, is a massive willow-tree which has an unusual history.

In a book entitled "James Austen Leigh", a Memoir by his daughter in 1911, she relates:-

"There was one tree in which he took special interest. This was a tall willow with a double stem, standing at the edge of the river in the middle of the garden bank. He had found it in 1852 a mere stake, stuck into the ground to support the end of a paling between Mr. Levett's garden and meadow. When removing the paling to enlarge the garden, he observed that the stake had taken root and was throwing out leaves. He left it and by careful pruning trained it to become a fine tree, though not without difficulty, for it had a chequered career. At one time it fell nearly prostrate owing to its roots being undermined by flood-water. Our father resolved to save it if possible and had it raised up, placing props beneath it to keep it upright. His family thought this a forlorn hope, and (my brother) Augustus named the tree "Vespasian", he being the Emperor who was determined to die standing, and as "Vespasian" it was afterwards known."

In 1956 the first occupant was Major Grieves. In 1970 it was bought by General McGill.

BERKELEY'S. From a manuscript book of records left by Mr. Austen Leigh we read:-

"To the house I added five bedrooms, over the three rooms which had been built by Mr. Levett. I made the passage upstairs communicating between the front and back staircase, and other alterations in and about the house."

This would suggest that the ground floor rooms were added between 1826 and 1853 (the part immediately adjoining Tudor House being removed in 1954). "The passage upstairs" is remembered today by one who had to sweep it, and the bedrooms beyond. The original staircase is still in use, though in a different position and without bannisters. Within the wall between the garage and dining-room a long glass window has been bricked-in.

In the reconstruction all the flooring (in the ground floor) was raised 18 inches, reducing the height of the rooms to more modern proportions.

The present sitting-room used to be the dining-room. On one wall hangs the portrait, as a young girl, of an ancestress of mine. When reading old family papers I came across the

Berkeley's – Vicarage

statement that she "had spent the summer with her uncle, the Vicar of Bray." It is strange to think of her taking her meals in this room! Was it she who insisted we *must* buy this particular house – that strange compulsion which made us select this out of all the others we had seen – who knows?

We were the first occupants, in 1956. It was named after one of the vicars, George Berkeley (who never lived in it) in this way. On the sale prospectus it was called Regency House, but being in close proximity to Tudor House some other name seemed more bearable. The Electricity Company refused to supply power to an un-named building so I rushed round to the church to find a surname of a vicar who had (I thought) lived here – and chose Berkeley. The requisite forms could then be properly filled in and signed, and we got our electricity!

Among the listed conditions of sale is one forbidding the playing of musical instruments while any church service is in progress (not even harps?!)

Additions we have made are the workshop over the garage in 1956, and the small study on the south end of the house in 1966. The architect employed is not responsible for its odd proportions. Our then neighbours objected to its being any higher lest it obstruct their view of the river.

During the excavation of the sun-trap in the lawn we found an Hungarian silver coin of 1872. Had somebody been on holiday there, or done the Grand Tour of Europe?

In 1957, while we were digging up our flower-bed backing onto St. Michaels Hall, we unearthed many bones and human skulls. The dustbin seemed the best place for them, but I retained one skull. It remained in a kitchen cupboard until November 1972, when I took it to Reading Museum. After inspection and tests by their expert it was pronounced:-

> "The skull of a late middle-aged woman. She ate stone-ground flour which would have contained gritty particles, hence the level horizontal wearing-away of the teeth. Period? Saxon."

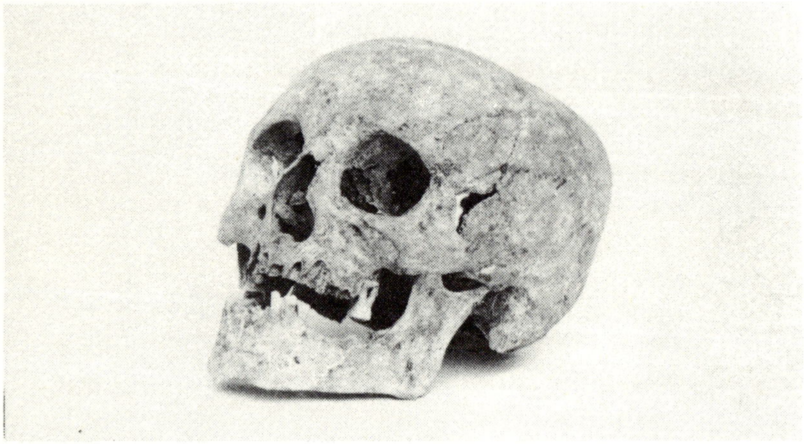

Skull

Standing in the drive-way here it might be as well to quote Mr. Austen Leigh's account of it:

> "Making the carriage-road, with the plantation in front of Chauntry House. Hitherto the only access to the Vicarage

House had been through the Church yard to the door in the wall; nor was there any other way of bringing a carriage from the stable yard to the house than by taking it round the Church yard to the same door. Some contrivance was required in making this road. There was only just room to bring it round the corner between the church yard and the Cowhouses and only just room for a carriage to turn opposite the Hall door. The advantage however was great, both from the increased convenience to the inhabitants of the house, and from rendering the Church yard less public. A considerable piece of land thus cut off from the meadow I gave to the parish for additional burial ground. This was consecrated by Bishop Wilberforce, October 23 1853, being a Sunday."

The original gate still stands in the corner of the drive to Tudor House.

THE WICKETS, so called for its view of the Cricket Club, was formed from "the brick stables" built by Rev. Austen Leigh. These were 4 horse-stalls and a small room at the river-end which was probably a harness-room. From 1938–1955 Mr. F. Jones rented it from the Vicar, for storing groceries, wines etc for his shop. He had to put wire-netting across the top to prevent rats demolishing the stores.

In 1955 it was re-made with the addition at the church end of a kitchen, bathroom, and garage, and has been the country home of Mr. Percy Myers.

Several large trees in the garden still stand, the oldest being the massive yew-tree beside the river. With the willow "Vespasian" they form a handsome, complementary though contrasting scene.

There is an old water trough still attached, on the garden side, to the original brick wall which joins on to:-

THE OLD COACH HOUSE, which is correctly named. Always two-storeyed, and a hay-loft above. When Mr. Victor Benjamin bought the estate he had this house built as a week-end home, and called it "The Olde Vic House" being a play on his name and the old vicarage. In 1959 he added, to his garden, part of the garden of "Merrimans", including the boat-house. That year he sold house and garden to Mr. P. Butler, who re-named it.

The original building had additions of the study and a small kitchen, which was enlarged in 1971, prior to the sale of the house to its present owners.

Before leaving this area, Mr. Austen Leigh's description of the whole grounds, from 1836–1954, may be of interest.

The kitchen-garden was made from "meadow and orchard, with a few fine elms, extending from the public footpath to the river. I threw into lawn the frontage towards the river, with the elms . . . By this means the frontage toward the river was trebled, and the whole reach of the river towards the lock was brought into view from the house. Before this was done, the lawn was very narrow, and when the Mulberry was in leaf very little of the water could be seen. The shrubbery on the north and east sides of the kitchen-garden were chiefly planted with shrubs."

ST. MICHAELS HALL

Marked on every map as "Chauntry of the Blessed Virgin 1330", this is one of the oldest buildings in Bray. It may even be coeval with the first church on this site.

Mr. Michael Bayley, A.R.I.B.A. Dipl. Arch. Oxford holds the theory that there used to be a Saxon (heathen) temple at Bilders Wells (i.e. the corner of Monkey Island Lane and A.308) which was dedicated to Hecate, the Goddess of the Dead. On it would have been her "sign" in the form of a dog, sacred to her, and her messenger.

With the coming of Christianity the monks sought to build a church, and collected the materials for it, but the legend is that every morning they found the stones had been removed by the Devil to the present site. Presumably they eventually gave up the struggle and built here. The theory then proceeds with the suggestion that the old stone depicting a dog was incorporated in the Chauntry since this, too, was a place for praying for the dead and would have provided a link readily understood by illiterate converts. Naming it only the "Chauntry of the Blessed Virgin", omitting the Mary, would also minimise the difficulty.

It is believed there was a priest for the Chauntry as well as a vicar for the church, though in 1546 Henry VIII's commission of enquiry into ecclesiastical matters reported "ther ys in the same parishe above the nombre of 700 housling people and no priests but the said chauntre priests." It was his duty "to celebrate the dyvyne survyce within ye parishe church of Braye, and Sondrye tymes in the year to provyde certayn duties which he doth accordingly."

The Bray Chauntry possessed no ornaments or goods of its own, using only those of the parish. It was "worth £14-0-7d of which 13s 2d came to the poor" who lived in a nearby almshouse (Chauntry House site). Here the priest acted as chaplain and distributed relief to the bedesmen.

Thus it continued until Henry VIII's dissolution activities. As there is no recorded date of the departure of Rev. Woodward, then vicar, it seems likely that both he and the Chauntry priest were evicted at this period. The building then became a drying and storage place for fishermen's nets until about 1682, when William Cherry took it over and converted it into a schoolroom and library for the free education of 20 poor boys.

He enclosed the east end with panelling and made a cottage for the schoolmaster from the two floors. The main hall became the school.

Kerry relates that he got into financial difficulties "several years before his death . . . in 1705" and was unable to continue the charitable enterprise. The school continued, however, as fee-paying until the opening of Braywick School in 1819.

The building then reverted to the Church and was used

for many purposes, ecclesiastical and otherwise. The cottage continued to house tenants, including at one time the village policeman.

The hall was regularly used for their meetings by the parish "Overseers", the precursors of the Bray Parish Council formed in 1894, who still meet there today.

It was known as 'The Old Schoolroom' until the late 1960's when, sad to say, it was re-named "St. Michaels Hall."

In 1959 the last tenant of the cottage end, Mr. Clinch, left. The church then refurbished the whole building, revealing the handsome piscina at the east end where the Chauntry altar would have stood. With the exception of the time-honoured tradition of Parish Council meetings, the whole building is now used solely for the church activities, e.g. Sunday school, youth group, C.E.M.S. etc.

Beside the Hall are toilets constructed in 1961. Previously there had been a shed housing the Bray fire-engine. In a 'Directory' of 1899 it is said to have been given to Bray in 1737 by "Lady Colleraine of Canon Hill," no doubt a generous and practical gift at the time, but by 1961 it had become a "museum piece", and it was sent to the Reading Museum, on loan from the Bray Parish Council who were responsible for it.

VICARAGE WALK

RIVERSIDE is built on what was an island. In the 1819 map it is marked "Geo. White". By 1887 we find the landward side of the river is reduced to a small stream, and there is a "fish weir and waterfall" beside the bank, which have disappeared by 1897 when 3 small islands in mid-stream are recorded. These probably increased in size until they joined to form one island, well known in living memory, of which more elsewhere.

There used to be two watering places for cattle grazing

on Gaskins (or Garstons) Mead (now the Sports Club). One was at the Fisheries end, early incorporated in the property, the other, between Riverside and Little Basing, was bought by the present owner in 1962.

In the same year he had bought all of the Sports Club land most of which was re-sold to them, but minus the land forming the drive from the main road to his house, which he retained.

The house was built in 1938. In 1957 he bought it from a Mr. Birn.

In the early years of the century there used to be a houseboat, the Shamrock, moored to the bank here. Later, it was accidently burned out.

LITTLE BASING was the first house to be built along here, in 1920. A long heap of river-dredging had to be removed first. It had been a popular pastime for the children to play over it, and they naturally regretted its going. Some of it was used as building material. At the moment the house is being considerably altered for its new owners.

MERRIMANS is approached through a brick-pillared entrance. When first built, in 1921, it was called "Pro Tem". Its garden extended to the Vicarage and included the boat-house now in the Old Coach House. It was sold, by Giddy and Giddy, in 1922 for its London owner, and renamed.

In 1961 most of the land was sold and the following year there were built on it RIVERHOLME and THAMESIDE HOUSE.

Until 1919 this (Merrimans) land had contained pigstyes, haystacks, and cow-houses for Good's dairy-herd which grazed on Gaskins Mead, the whole area being rented from the Vicar.

LYCH GATE AND ST. MICHAEL'S COTTAGE

Lich is an Old English word meaning "field of the dead,"

hence the proximity of every Lychgate to a church, or churchyard.

This one is at least 500 years old, since there can be seen carved in an upright timber under the arch the date 1448 in Arabic numerals.

In a deed of 1763 it is referred to as a "public house commonly called or known by the name of 'The Six Bells'," and is being rented to John Stokes by Richard Tonson, "for one year on payment of one peppercorn."

From 1684 to 1857 it changes hands, either by sale or as rented property, many times, being referred to variously as a public-house and as a private dwelling.

In a deed of 1839 it is rented "for one peppercorn" to the Vicar, the Rev. Walter Levett.

From the Rev. Austen Leigh's Mss of 1853, "On this site formerly stood a public-house called 'The Six Bells.' These premises were purchased, in 1839, by the Rev. Walter Levett, then Vicar of Bray; who took down the building thereon, and erected the present tenements. Mr. Levett resigned the Vicarage in October 1852 and in December of the same year, he conveyed the premises to three Trustees, for the following purposes.

1. That the two large rooms, to which the open staircase leads, should be occupied by "Two poor persons, inhabitants of the Parish of Bray," to be appointed by a majority of the Trustees, and to be removable at their discretion.

2. That the remainder of the house, with the adjoining garden, be let to a tenant, and that the rent be invested for the purpose of keeping the whole in repairs.

3. That the Trustees be not obliged to keep in repair the wooden tiled shed in the garden.

4. That the Vicar, for the time being, have the option of renting the said premises, for six pounds a year.

The Trustees first appointed were the Rev. Js Edward Austen Leigh (Vicar), John Jeane Coney Esq. of Braywick Grove, John Hibbert Esq. of Braywick Lodge.

On the decease of Mr. Coney, in 1862, E. H. Palmer Esq. of

Canon Hill was appointed Trustee in his place.

The Trust Deed is deposited in the Parish Chest, and a copy of it is entered in the Vestry Book."

The legal estate was vested in the official Trustee of Charities, by Order dated 25th July 1862.

In general, it has since been the home of couples or single persons, some of whom have worked for the church, e.g. vergers, cleaners.

Since 1958 St. Michael's Cottage has been rented by the Vicar, continuing an option specified in the deeds, who has used it for employees at the Vicarage, and church.

The Bray Parish Council records of 1903, list repairs to the copper and two cesspools; the pump; and the Archway. In 1952, a special fund was set up for restorations, which were completed to the exterior by 1955.

In 1966 radiators were installed in both dwellings and "all mod. cons," made life easier for the inhabitants.

In the Lychgate flat the accommodation today consists of a double bedroom, sitting-room-cum-kitchen, bathroom and toilet, plus a ground-floor room which is seldom used.

St. Michael's Cottage has a sitting-room, dining-room, double bedroom, kitchen and bathroom.

Both have massive old beams but are light and cheerful.

They remain in the hands of the Charity Commissioners, termed "Levett's Charity" and continue to be administered by the Bray Parish Council.

CHURCH LANE

Town planning being non-existent until recently, villages as a collection of buildings tended to develop outwards from one central point. This was often the church.

In our own case we find the oldest cottages near the lychgate on the direct line joining Upper Bray Road to the church – a road which can claim almost as much antiquity as the road from Windsor to Braywick.

Church Lane was at one time known as St. Thomas's Street, for which I can find no reason other than the imaginative one of his being the patron saint of some of the early clergy. Three vicars bearing the name came and left within the period 1443 to 1454, the last being Thomas Luyde during whose time here the lychgate was built.

An early advertisement for the Hinds Head claims it as being of 15th century origin, so maybe we can give the lane a similar date.

If we start there and look around, we find a row of cottages on our right. The first, LYCH GATE COTTAGE, is very small. Until 1960 it consisted of only one bedroom and one living room, with a tiny cooking area behind it. It used to be "No.4". Beside it is YEW TREE COTTAGE, No.3, slightly larger with two floors. In the yard behind it was the communal wash-copper.

Then we find DORMER COTTAGE. Here lives Mrs. Plumridge to whom I am indebted for much information for this book. Her father, Mr. Jesse Gay, owned these cottages in 1927, and she came here in 1932.

It is larger than its neighbours, having two rooms downstairs and an extension of kitchen, and a bathroom behind. For eight years she kept the inside of the church clean and bright.

Next to this there used to be "No.5" but this was incorporated into the Hinds Head in the early 1930's which, in its turn, was originally two cottages, at right-angles to the others.

At one time all on this side of the lane were called Church Cottages, while the opposite side was, and officially still is, Lych Cottages. At the back of the end one is still No.4 approached from, but not visible from, the lane.

On this side, near the gate, is THE LIMES. The present house was built in 1936. Here there had previously been a house of the same name, but somewhat smaller, of Georgian architecture. The map of 1819, while showing all the other cottages, leaves this site open so one may surmise its arrival after that date. Mrs. Whalley was its owner at the beginning of the century. She was well known for her excellent laundry-work, and also gave lodging to any unmarried curates in the parish. In common with all the then "older generation" she was affectionately called "Granny Whalley" by the youngsters.

Now we start on a whole line of cottages.

The first four of these have now (1972) been transformed into two dwellings, at present unnamed.

During their reconstruction I enquired of the foreman whether he had found any large fireplace, or some such, which would substantiate a report I had received that there used to be maltings there. "No", says he, "none like that. But it *would* account for the amount of grain we found among the floorboards and other wood-work." Unfortunately it was too late in the operation to collect any of it for analysis as to age, but one may validly suppose it was connected with "The Six Bells Inn" at the lychgate.

These erstwhile four cottages were known latterly as Gay's cottages. Mr. Jesse Gay, and after him his son Mr. Sid Gay owned them, and carried on a flourishing business as builders, carpenters and plumbers at the fourth cottage, where there was a good, square yard for materials and the lorry. This yard at one time contained the communal wash-copper for all the cottages on that side. The water had to be drawn up in a bucket from a well. If it was your turn to have a wash-day you prayed for fine weather!

A further amalgamation of three cottages produced THE COTTAGE next door. The conversion, carried out in lavish style, took place about 1960.

The next two houses are officially listed as Nos. 2 and 1 Oldfield View. They must have adopted this name from the ability to see "Oldfield", a name still used by some to denote Bray Green, the common-land by the Causeway. In the photograph of the Green we can just see these cottages at the back.

Next to No. 1 is THE RINGERS, an inn obviously as old as

its neighbours and possibly in use as such when "The Six Bells" reverted to private occupancy – but that is guesswork again.

There used to be two more cottages on this row, but they were pulled down in 1904 when Ferry End was built.

CHURCH DRIVE

RED TILES was built in 1882 for Miss Rouquette, who lived there until her death in 1940. It replaced two old cottages which had faced onto Church Drive for, probably, two centuries. The house bore no name during her lifetime. This was not unusual, as many houses were known only by their owners' names. After her death it was called "Chauntry Lodge" until some 17 years ago, when it became "Red Tiles."

Red Tiles

The property comprised the whole rectangle between the Hinds Head and Church Drive, taking in her stables and coach-house (now Green Shutters) and the old cottage on the corner.

She found the garden inadequate to her needs, so rented part of the garden of Vicarage Cottage from the Vicar. In a dome a-top the house there used to be a bell which was rung by a bell-pull in the kitchen punctually at 8.30 each morning. Whether there was a domestic reason we know not, but it served to alert the local children to their need to go off to school, in Hibbert Rd!

Miss Rouquette lived in Bray for 58 years and is remembered today for her many services to the village and the church, and for her great kindness to her staff. Shortly before she died she walked slowly but determinedly, in her slippers, to visit her ex-gardener who lay ill in The Terrace. From 1903 she provided a happy home here for an orphaned nephew and niece and it was the niece who started the first Girl Guide Company in Bray. Today the nephew remembers her warmly as "a very remarkable person – very."

In 1971 the interior was re-arranged to admit more light and to modernise the kitchen area. The garage was built, replacing a rickety wooden shed.

THE OLD COTTAGE on the corner was never occupied during Miss Rouquette's time. It had its upstairs rooms, and a square baker's oven and chimney which protruded onto the pathway. The village children of the first decade of this century enjoyed chasing each other around it, without let or hindrance from its owner.

On her death, a Mrs. Orr bought the whole property. Having retained a part of the garden for the cottage she sold the house. By this time the cottage was decrepit and had a tree growing through it and out of its roof. She remade it internally, and let it to various tenants. The last to rent it were Bakels Limited, of Slough who eventually bought it in 1966 and still use it for visiting employees or guests from abroad.

The stables and coach-house she used to store, and sometimes sell, antique furniture.

This is now GREEN SHUTTERS, strictly speaking in the High Street but its early history belongs to Miss Rouquette. Over the stable she had built bedrooms and a bathroom for the cook, with her son, plus a small living room and even smaller, 5ft, kitchen at the back, at ground level.

The small garden was given an illusion of space by the open-work wrought-iron party-wall, now replaced by solid bricks, by Bakels.

The building underwent considerable alterations from 1969–71. The stable and sitting-room were opened out by removing the wall and chimney to create the modern lounge, with a large new fireplace. An open staircase leads up to the two bedrooms and bathroom. The large kitchen-dining-room with plate glass window-wall is both light and spacious, incorporating the old and tiny kitchen and extending beyond it. The owner and his wife participated in the actual building of it all. The old coach-house at present remains a storage area. The bottle-glass in the front window was specially made-to-order.

During the building operations an unexploded 28 pound German bomb was exposed in the garden, and had to be taken away by Army experts!

BRAY HIGH STREET

The entrance to the village, from the Maidenhead end, is at a small bridge – Hog, or Hogge Bridge it is called. It traverses a dry ditch now but there used to be a full stream running under it. This came from Hibbert Road, near Green Lane, curving round the boundary of the Sports Club, and joining the Thames at Sawkins Bridge. It is thought by some that it could have been a flax-washing-ditch, which is partly substantiated by an old deed which records that flax formed part of the tithes, in 1341, and would have had to be cleaned in a fast-running stream. There were osier-beds each side of Hibbert Road as late as 1821, so flax could well have grown there too. The line of the stream still forms the Maidenhead Borough Boundary.

Over Hogge Bridge, then. The repair of its fencing is a constantly recurring expense to the Council, due to ill-judged driving of lorries and cars.

The path on this side was built-up and surfaced in the 1960's. Previously a narrow, irregular, and pitted bank beside the ditch, it threatened twisted ankles and certainly could not accommodate a pram.

The first building is a bungalow, THE ORCHARD, built nearly a hundred years ago. Its garden ablaze with bulbs in the spring makes an attractive introduction to the village. Its owner in the '60s used to deck the fir tree with fairy-lights at Christmas, and an even earlier one, Mrs. Armitage, gave a Christmas-tree party to the children of the village sending them home clutching the presents from the tree. The garden abuts on BRAY GREEN, the only open space the village possesses.

In 1819 it was termed "Bray Common Allotment," and was available to sixteen specified householders or their tenants for pasturage of one cow per person. Somewhere along the line it became the responsibility of the Parish Council who virtually acquired "squatters rights." A rough, uneven, and seasonally muddy area, it was nevertheless, valued by energetic children and dog-owners. In 1966-68 there was a nationwide registration of Common Land, and Bray Parish Council hastened to include Bray Green in the list. Now no longer limited, legally, to a mere sixteen people, all can enjoy it. In 1970 the Parish Council had it dug up, levelled, and re-grassed. The twelve trees planted on the East and South sides were donated by local residents. Those on the East are forest trees; on the South, small decorative. On the part adjoining the Causeway footpath the fenced-off area is specially raised and strengthened for the parking of cars.

Bray – Early Thirties

During this century it has been the scene of many jollifications. Fairs with swings, roundabouts, and stalls; celebrations after Bray Regattas; and carnivals – especially the Carnival in 1921. That was an event to crown all events, according to local memories.

Let me take you behind the scenes about this.

I visited several "senior citizens" in quest of Bray's 20th century history, taking along a small tape-recorder with an unobtrusive microphone, and asking for information.

My first port of call was at Jesus Hospital. After some hour's talk I asked, "Is there anything you remember, particularly, about any events in the village?"

"Oh yes" she replied with enthusiasm. "There was a carnival. Mrs. Earle, at The Old Dutch House, organised it. There was a fancy dress competition and I won 1st prize. I was a Victorian girl, with a basket of posies." It had obviously been a great day for her.

A week later another family very kindly gave me an

evening's-worth of information. I asked the same question. "Oh yes," answered one, "There was a carnival . . . I won 1st prize". "Are you sure?" I queried. "Mrs. X won 1st prize." "I did, you know. I was a pirate. I won the boys' prize."

Ten days later, another part of the village the same scene, the same question. "Oh yes . . . and I was a cowboy. I think I got a prize."

Another week and I was at The Terrace. The questions were becoming routine by now, including the final one – "Oh yes . . . and I was a shepherdess. Why are you laughing?"

"Sorry," I said, "but don't tell me you got a prize!"

"But I did," she replied. "I got 3rd prize."

Many others remember that day. Bray had never seen anything like it – bunting, flags, flowers – gaiety everywhere. Fancy dress for all who chose to wear it, hired from London at Mrs. Earle's expense; Thomas's Fair on the Green. In Mrs. Earle's house one man kept watch over parked coats and wraps. He wore a large false moustache, a hat pulled well down and an overcoat. He was a local man, but surely all would take him for a specially employed detective? The streets filled during the evening as the houses spilled out their occupants to swell the throng. A baby was christened that morning and was proudly carried, in her christening robe, by the mother at the head of a procession which paraded round the roads, through the garden of Old Dutch House and out again. Costumes were judged and prizes awarded. Off, then to the Green for the fun and the food.

By happy coincidence (and coincidence it was – there was no collusion) a society wedding took place in the church in the afternoon. Smart chauffeur-driven cars disgorged flowered chiffons, laces and silks with their black or grey-toppered escorts. The bride arrived to the accompaniment of admiring oohs and aahs from the crowd lining the route – a crowd which grew longer and deeper, jockeying for good positions from which to see the wedding party when they left. The bells pealed, excited necks stretched forward, small children were restrained by their elders and the bridal car started off. At the High Street four "Beef-eater" costumed young men formed up ahead of it and led the procession. Others danced and laughed around, slowing the progress to walking-pace until the bridge at Jesus Hospital was reached, the crowd parted, and waved the party on to Holyport. It was a spontaneous outburst, a joyous addition to an already gay occasion. Happy the bride and happy the village.

At sunset, matches and tapers lit up the night-lights in the glass jars slung on gates, windows and branches. Dancing on the green, dancing in the streets, dancing on Mrs. Earle's lawn and round Holman's Mat, until the showmen of the fair silenced their great machines, and the music.

And so to bed.

Truly a day to remember fifty years on.

Back then to a more sober look at today. Facing the Green are two houses on land owned in 1817 by the See of Oxford, and built in 1956, WESTERING COTTAGE and CAUSEWAY COTTAGE. Now that the Green is registered, they should enjoy their open outlook "in perpetuity."

The Causeway's origins are unknown. It was obviously constructed to allow of access from Braywick to Bray across the water meadows without getting one's feet wet, and must, from time to time, have been repaired and also heightened. Known by some as "King Charles's Causeway" and by the children of 1900 as "the cast" nobody can give any reason for either name. Some say it was made by residents of Canon Hill House to allow of their walking dry-shod to church – but again no date is mentioned. It appears on every map, whether O.S. or privately produced, as a public pathway and bridlepath raised above the surrounding fields, and with trees on both sides.

Going up it from Bray, the first bridge used to cross

sunken meadows which were frequently under water. On its far side was a much deeper part always known as "Nokes' Hole," and always named in fear and horror. The story went that one, Nokes, was going home the worse for liquor late at night, and fell into the hole "and drowned himself." The tougher youngsters would stop and peer into it, hoping maybe Nokes could still be seen!

The second bridge crossed a stream flowing from the Maidenhead side to join what was then the Cut below "the tumbling bay," where the stream from Canon Hill formed a small waterfall. Today the lower stream is dry except in exceptionally wet weather, and the Cut has been re-routed to pass under the first bridge, remade on its way to Maidenhead.

There are still some old and fine trees on the right-hand side, and saplings generated from the felled trees on the left are bidding fair to replace their forebears. The dreaded Dutch Elm disease has not struck here, so far.

The water-meadows no longer provide the show of flowers so much enjoyed by earlier generations – kingcups, bog-irises, meadowsweet, cowslips and others – and the birds and butterflies appropriate to such conditions have gone too. Such is the price for keeping Bray safe from the extensive flooding of yesteryear.

The fields are now for grazing cattle and horses; the Causeway is the only semi-rural area for taking a stroll, and still provides safe passage for pedestrians both from damp feet and from motorists.

Back, then to the High Street. Today it extends from here to The Crown, but it used to be "West Street" as far as The Ringers. On the opposite side is a large house standing behind many handsome old forest trees, CHAUNTRY HOUSE. There may well have been a small building here from the 14th century. The priest at the old chauntry chapel had part of his salary specifically allocated "to the poore of the paryshe" who would have included homeless wanderers needing board and lodging on their way to everywhere and nowhere.

In 1504 and in 1597 according to Kerry, it was owned by Henry Norres (Norris) of Ockwells Manor but there is no description of its purpose then.

In 1549 it had been "an ancient hostelry termed 'The Chauntyre' " kept by Thomas Horme. A certain Hugo Tanner reported him for keeping a "Tenys-play", which he is commanded to remove from the house. Later he tries running a "Bowlyngalye" within his premises but gets a rap over the knuckles for that too. Not being a social historian, I can give no reason for the legal wet-blanketing of what would appear to be some harmless amusements.

A small parchment document of 1705 can be broadly translated thus:-

"Louis Grove of Bray, clothworker of the first part, leases to John Longutt, The Chauntry or Chauntry House or by whatsoever name or names in Bray Town, connected with the Chauntry of the Blessed Virgin Mary, at a peppercorn rent to be paid at Michaelmas."

There is now a gap of nearly 150 years.

The date 1753 is still visible high up on the house at the north end. Maybe this large brick building was added to the smaller one – we cannot be certain. Such a large building may have been the start of its being a workhouse, for it is so called in the Inclosure Award of 1817. There it is mentioned as forming one of the boundaries to the field Gaskins Mead (now the Sports Club). At that time the house was in the shape of a reversed F.

By 1875 we find the south end built out to join the central area of the F which would account for its being known later as "the new wing", with a large bathroom and bedroom.

In 1861, says Kerry, it belonged to a Mrs. Williams. Subsequently two generations named Lewis owned it, the second letting it to Mr. Leslie Lloyd Bailey until 1910.

Mr. Heath (from The Terrace) was caretaker there for two years, 1908–10, and his daughter remembers well the spooky cellars. They contained two cells with gratings and spiked iron doors (for miscreants?) also some long slate slabs where, it was reported, the dead were laid out. These cellars were deep in water during flood-times, necessitating high wading-boots for her father when he went to fetch coal etc. In the kitchen there was a long and solid wooden table, said to have been there since the workhouse days.

There were two greenhouses in the grounds, one large and one, nearer the church wall, small. The latter contained the boiler. When digging below it, a number of human bones were uncovered. Mr. Heath notified the Vicar who had them "vetted" in case there had been foul play. However all was well, and they were re-buried in situ. No mention was made of their age or period.

During the first world war the family Nicholson was in residence.

About 1920 Lady Benson left a troubled Ireland for the calmer atmosphere of Bray. She obtained permission to make a gateway from her garden to the church, a privilege which lasted until the Church authorities, in their perambulation of their property in 1958, insisted upon its closure. She was the first President of the Women's Institute in 1928, and is recorded as having been at the funeral of Miss Rouquette (Red Tiles) in 1940.

Twenty-three years ago it was bought for conversion into flats and continued thus until 1965 when the ground-floor of the newer part became the display-area for antiques, large and small. The smaller end plus the old large kitchen remained as a home for the owner.

Above there are three large and three small flats.

In the grounds there were stables, built about 1800. These are now THE DOWER HOUSE. It was converted soon after the last war, and sold to Humphrey Lestoq, better known to the general public as "Flying Officer Kite" from his part in a popular radio programme of those days. With the exception of an enlargement of the originally tiny kitchen in the late '60s it remains as originally designed.

The high flint wall opposite encloses CHAUNTRY COTTAGE

which originally housed the gardener to the big house, the garden producing vegetables and fruit, and extending to the Causeway and along it as far as Causeway Cottage's boundary. The cottage is of 14th century origin, having but two small rooms at first. The windows were set flush with the walls, their extensions being added in 1961. About the same time an additional wing was built on the south-east side, also the garage. The garden is a tribute to its owner's care and attention providing a mass of bloom throughout the seasons.

The next house used to be called "Aleyn" in recognition of the famous "Vicar of Bray", Simon Aleyn. It is now "No. 1" (High St.). It was built about 1890 by the energetic Mrs. Woodhouse who did so much in, for, and with the village and her family. At one time it was the dairy selling the milk from the herd which grazed Garstons Mead and the fields behind the Hinds Head. The door at the back of the house, where the milk was handed over, has since been blocked-up. Externally the house remains as built, likewise its front garden wall with its decorative cast-iron railings.

As late as 1960 one could still see the cattle being driven from the Hibbert Road fields to this narrow lane. At the bottom there is a house over-looking open fields beyond.

JUNIPERS was re-named recently. In 1911 Mrs. Woodhouse built it for her own occupation, and called it "The Nest." It has been modernised and "tidied-up" by its present owner, but retains the atmosphere of its origins.

DELAPOLE is the third of Mrs. Woodhouse's additions to the village. It was built soon after "Aleyn", about 1900. Whether it is a coincidence or not, I do not know – but a Sir Richard Delapole once owned "The Old Cottage" on the opposite corner, and sold it to Miss Rouquette (of Red Tiles Chauntry Lodge). It was for a short time divided into two flats, but is a whole dwelling again today.

HANOVER HOUSE, and HANOVER COTTAGE were originally one house, called "The Cedars". It appears as such on all the old maps and is thought to date from the early 18th century.

It has had several owners and many lessees. Two names well known in the village's records have been Lewis and Woodhouse the latter being two aunts of the energetic builder and farmer, living there in the mid-nineteenth century, and a descendant of theirs being in the cottage section today.

It was divided into its present portions in 1957, when the small porticos over the front-doors were added. Some modernisation internally has taken place, and garages added at the end of the building but the structure, including old beams within, remains unaltered – neat lines in red brick and an unbroken line of tiled roof over the two homes.

Across the next drive-way is the Hinds Head Coffee Room, an account of which appears in another chapter.

Beside it we find petrol pumps and BRAY GARAGE. Where the pumps stand today there used to be four old cottages of much the same period as the others in this part of the village. They had small gardens behind them with the usual communal washing-copper. Like all the High Street Cottages their ground-floors were below road-level and suffered considerably in times of floods. They differed at first floor level in that they had dormer windows instead of the flush-fronts of the others. We will see them disappear in the course of the history of the garage.

The seeds of this could be said to have been sown in 1922 when the West brothers started a coach-service – one coach was garaged in the barn behind Bray Cottage (now the Coffee Room) and another in the Vicarage garage (now Old Coach House).

Taxis for hire were in the Hinds Head garage, previously stables and now the dining-room built in Barry Neame's time. By 1927 they needed more accommodation and bought from Mr. Todd "Thames House" where Baker Marks had produced his famous soda-cakes and bread early in the century. It had tall wooden doors leading to the garden and yard at the back. At this time the petrol was dispensed from a pump right on the pavement, which must have been inconvenient for pedestrians. The logical development was to buy, and demolish, the four old cottages, incorporating their gardens with the land behind Thames House, thus providing a good large garage-yard. The old pumps were removed and new ones installed where we see them today. This happened in 1930. The large shed at the far end of the yard was erected over a previous sunken-garden. During the last war it was used for assembling parts for tanks and aircraft. With the return of peace the Wests reverted to their coaches, running a coach/bus service until 1968. The following year the car showroom was constructed from some of the rooms of Thames House.

Today they carry out repairs, garage cars for residents, provide a taxi-service, and supply petrol from the pumps.

The old house is "feeling its age" and may well need a major operation ere long.

Next to the garage is MORRELL's. The name "Thames House" was over the door until very recently, this being the erstwhile front entrance, when it had a canvas canopy on metal struts which could be lowered to provide shade for the baker's shop.

For many years it was run by Mr. Marks, whose granddaughter still lives in the village. Memories of those who were children in the early 1900's are uniformly of a handsome and kindly old man with a long white beard. One little girl, who attended Sunday School regularly, used to gaze at him, wide-eyed, thinking he was Moses! His bread and soda-cakes are reported to have been excellent and his readiness to help by roasting Sunday dinners in his ovens is remembered with gratitude. In those days there were three solid hitching-posts for horses set into the pavement's edge and the pavement itself was of cobblestones.

Ever since the Wests bought it this part has been let as one or another business. For a short time in the '30's it was tobacconist and newsagent. In the '50's it was "Marjorie", a ladies hairdresser's Some four years ago a Mr. Morell took over the sub-post office from Mr. Jones, combining it with confectionery, tobacconist, and newsagent. He left in 1970, and it is now run by a local resident with assistance from others from the village. It can be said to cater for all age-groups. At the post-office area the senior citizens collect their weekly pensions; parents the family allowance for their children; everybody their stamps and postal requirements. Newspapers, magazines, postcards and greetings-cards are on sale, and the children can be seen in the afternoons, on their return from school, buying sweets and iced-lollies from the freezing cabinet. The newspaper delivery-round necessitates collection from Maidenhead about 5.30 a.m. in order to provide customers with the latest news to read with their breakfasts.

Beside the shop, and standing a little back from the road is RICKHAMS. This is a charming house which has also been called "Thames Cottage" and "River Near" during this century. The present name appears in Kelly's Directory for 1929 when a Captain Simpson lived there. It is thought that the rear wing was part of an old Tudor Cottage, and that the frontage was added in the eighteenth century. The kitchen, the garage (previously coach-house) and the rooms above them were added in the 19th century. All passers-by have reason to be grateful for the cheering floral display in the front of the house during most of the year.

As there is no pavement from here, it is safer to look at the next three buildings from the bus-stop opposite – the traffic is a menace just here.

The high wall and the house are built with bricks left over from those used in the building of Brunel's famous railway-bridge at Maidenhead in the 19th century. The lights at the back-door are railway lights, so maybe the original owner was connected with the Great Western Railway! It was called "Bray Lodge" for many years, but the past 30-odd years it has been SARAH'S COTTAGE, named for its owner, Mrs. Sarah Savory. She re-named it because a house in The Fisheries was also Bray Lodge and it caused repeated difficulties with the postman. Its interior was spaciously planned and remains unaltered today.

You need to look carefully to spot the name of the next house, JERSEY COTTAGE. Its history is entirely linked with the shop next door of which it was a part until 1935. Its name was given as a memento of a happy holiday spent in Jersey. The garage used to be a bake-house adjoining the shop.

JONES SHOP. It has been in business for over 200 years. 1760 saw its opening by "Anne Jones, Dealer in Teas and Tobaccos" and it has remained in the same family ever since. A picture of the two original cottages of wattle-and-daub was painted as late as the 19th century, whether from reported memory or reality one cannot tell. It shows none of the buildings on the north, but that may just be artistic licence. Known dates are the 1760 opening and the rebuilding of 1935 which produced the building we see today – red brick and tiled roof. The many generations during the 200 years produced citizens with a lively sense of service to the community, one of them giving some 30 years to Parish Council work in his spare time. The sub-post-office was another activity of value to the village, especially in its early years when telegrams were tapped out by hand, received by transmitter and had to be delivered over rough roads on foot or by bicycle in all weathers, maybe even to Monkey Island. Letters and postcards were franked by hand, in the shop, with the postmark "BRAY" and later "BRAY – MAIDENHEAD."

Until electricity arrived the shop was lit by large hanging brass lamps. However, it scored two joint-firsts with the Hinds Head in having the first electric lights and the first telephones.

Local memories relate how "Uncle Tom" was always generous to the children who took their pennies, or halfpennies, to buy sweets. A twisted cone of paper would be filled by tipping the large glass-jar until the cone overflowed – whatever the size of the coin proffered in payment.

Both he and his small customers enjoyed the operation at the time, and the telling of the tale is accompanied by happy smiles some seventy years later.

The post-office chore was passed, in 1925, to Sealey's the grocer at the end of The Terrace, where it remained until the Bowlers handed over to Budgens who did not want it. The Jones family then took it on again until 1969. The present pillar letter-box dates from that time. Previously there was a box let into the end wall of the shop. In 1958 the storage-yard beside the shop was made from the original garden. Where the tall brick wall stands beside the road there was once a wooden fence and a hedge.

Today Mr. and Mrs. Fred Jones carry on the long tradition. One of their twin daughters lives with her husband and children in Jersey Cottage. Both daughters help, from time to time, in the shop. Deliveries by van to customers continues, and is much valued by them. The tradition of service to the community continues with Mr. Fred Jones' involvement with the Village Hall Club, of which he was chairman for many years, and Mrs. Jones deals with all the bookings for the Hall (no small task) and provides invaluable assistance on the Village Hall Committee, especially in the catering for the various social occasions.

On the opposite corner are SUNFLOWER COTTAGES owned by Mr. Fred Jones whose father owned them before him. A block of four small red-brick cottages, they were probably built in the 18th century. Behind them there used to be a well, which is now filled and covered. A communal wash-copper probably existed too.

The extensions at the back were added in 1933, and Mr. Jones plans to paint the brickwork in white this year.

Beside them are two very old houses. The first, called SHOTTERY, was probably two cottages. An indication of their age is provided by old beams on the ground floor. These are numbered, in Roman numerals, from I to VI which places them as dating around 1450. They were probably foresters' homes at that time. A modern kitchen and a room over it have been added, and a garage built in part of the old garden but the old rooms with their massive beams survive. For a few years, in the '60's, it was called Tudor Cottage, but has now reverted to the previous name.

Its immediate neighbour is STUART COTTAGE which would have been the third in the row. This is smaller but is obviously coeval. The wattle and daub, the old staircase and oak beams remain.

For some years, in the '60's, as the traffic increased in weight and numbers these old cottages suffered from noise and severe vibration. When the road was repaired in 1970 it was found that no proper foundation had ever been incorporated. This was rectified, the road re-laid, and today all is well. Double-glazing has also reduced the noise nuisance.

A later arrival is HOLLY COTTAGE, built about 1810–1820 and owned by another of the Jones family. Little is known of its history. It appears to have been one of the many of Bray's houses "to let", rather than having any long-term occupant. The reason for one side being a few feet wider than the other lies in a passage-way between it and The Old Dutch House having been incorporated into the cottage. A mere gap remains there today.

Now for THE OLD DUTCH HOUSE. It used to be called "Dormer Cottage" and was a farm-house fenced on its two long sides but with a brick wall at the "pointed end" which was the boundary of Hill House Farm. (The very short road did not exist until Brayfield Road was made, about 1910–11). In the farmyard there was a pond for the ducks.

One of its owners was a Holman, giving his name to the grassy plot on the north side (now occupied by the War Memorial); but no other early records have come to light. A painting of, possibly, about 1880 shows it as a typical picture-book farm cottage. With hens a-clucking, ducks a-quacking and a small girl probably asking innumerable "why's" of a busy mother, it gives an excellent atmosphere of activity and homeliness. Alas, the printer of this book pronounced it unsuitable for inclusion here. It is one of many pictures painted by a Mr. Smith who lived in Church Lane at the end of the last century.

Soon after, a Miss Holland bought it. Her nickname of "old Dutch" became attached to her house, much to her amusement. Since she also had a number of valuable Dutch tiles within it, it all seemed very appropriate. She let it, over a number of years, to various tenants.

One was Mrs. Campbell, a well-known actress, whose stage-name was Betty Balfour.

The small room in the garden used to be her music-room, where she and her producer would try out, or practise, new numbers for her shows. It had previously been a greenhouse.

In 1940 Miss Holland, who had by then become Mrs. Earle, sold it to a Mrs. Marks (no relation to Baker Marks) who stayed for seven years.

In 1947 Mr. and Mrs. Dill Russell bought it. The fence on the Ferry Road side was in a sorry state, and they replaced it with the present brick wall, painted white to harmonise with its surroundings. All the trees had grown uncomfortably large, causing a nuisance to passers-by, so they were trimmed back, but without spoiling their beauty. Those on the south side of the garden, horse-chestnuts, are a fine sight each Spring. A large tree on the High Street corner eventually had to come down as the heavy lorries and vans were constantly knocking it, and the base of the tree was extending into the road.

There is said to be an underground passage connecting the house with Jesus Hospital.

It is scheduled a Grade I building, so the exterior is subject to rigorous controls today. However, the interior has been totally reconstructed by its present owner, Lady Harrison-Hughes, who has never lived in it, and it is quite unrecognisable in cottage-terms. The lovely old chimney which supported the roof was scrapped, causing the roof to fall in, so even the exterior is somewhat changed, too. There are caretakers watching over its welfare, but it has not been inhabited for several years.

Miss Holland/Mrs. Earle was a remarkable lady. She was a great gambler who had phenomenally good luck and was well known in all gambling circles both in London and elsewhere.

At the fine old age of 92 years she went off in a chauffeur-driven car to Monte Carlo "to raise £5,000 to help put on a rally at the Albert Hall for old people." She reckoned it would take her only 10 days playing trente-et-quarante, "which is favourable to the punter." There were some casinos in the south of France which banned her – she was too expensive for them!

In Bray she was full of energy and goodwill. An account of the Carnival she organised in 1921 can be found elsewhere.

The only other buildings in the High Street are Jesus Hospital and Hanover Mead.

JESUS HOSPITAL. This building was completed in 1628, due to the benefaction of William Goddard in 1609. Though he died that year he had left in his will full instructions as to its building, financing, and purpose. This last was that it should house 40 poor people; it should have a chapel; the wardens of the Fishmongers' Company should be "governers for ever;" and that it should be called "Jesus Hospital."

For many years there were allowances of coal and wood, and of cloth, and small amounts of "spending money." Much has changed since then.

Today there are only 25 homes, housing some 30 people; a chaplain's house; and a matron's house similar to the others. All have been modernised with internal plumbing; cooking facilities instead of the original communal eating-place; a sit-in bath; free electricity and gas in lieu of the old fuel allotment; and gifts of money and soft sweets (a thoughtful touch!) at Christmas.

The Prime Warden of the Fishmongers' Company visits once a year, the Warden at Christmas, and the Secretary at

The Goddard Monument – Bray Church

The New Sanctuary, Free-standing Altar and Identical Ambos, 1968

Jesus Hospital, 1972

Hanover Mead, 1972

Bray – a View (pre 1904)

High Street, 1972

Village Hall – Old Porch, 1972

Village Hall – New Porch, 1973

Bray Green, 1972

Hibbert Road Cottages, 1972

other times during the year. Conditions of allocation remain the same, viz: a minimum age of 50 years; residence within the Parish of Bray for 20 years, or a connection with some member of the Fishmongers' Company.

Residents can tend their own gardens behind the houses if they wish, and there is a whole-time gardener in his own, modernised, house, to keep in order the communal land which is today entirely on the village side of the Cut.

The field at the back used to be known as "The Rec," or recreation ground. Here there were parties in the '14–'15 war for wounded soldiers and village participants; here there were Maypole celebrations; here some of the Jones family kept racing-pigeons; and here, beside the Cut, were banks of cowslips.

HANOVER MEAD. The Clothworkers' Company bought this field from the Fishmongers' Company in 1963. For centuries it had been grazed by cattle and formed a peaceful rustic scene at the entrance to the village.

They wanted to provide housing for elderly retired people and so, in conjunction with the Hanover Housing Association, planned and built these 18 self-contained units. There are 15 for two persons but the rest are for single occupancy. A communal laundry-room and a spare room for a guest add to the amenities, while a resident warden with a double flat is on-call from each unit should help be needed.

From the beginning of the project, Bray was given the opportunity of seeing and criticising the plans – a courtesy which was much appreciated locally. The design of the whole building was carefully considered so that it would harmonise with Jesus Hospital on the opposite side of the road. The gardens are mostly laid as lawns, for ease of upkeep. Some of the old trees on the site have been retained, and some new ones planted.

It was officially "opened" on October 11th 1971 by Mr. Charles S. Oliver, Master of the Clothworkers' Company.

The Hanover Housing Association is a charitable organisation providing housing for the elderly "from Perth to Plymouth," as they say. They expect to have some 2,500 units in occupation by the Spring of 1973. Financial support is provided for the building by local government bodies as well as private donations. Much more is needed, nationwide, and Bray is happy to have this local assistance for the problem.

The cost to the users is somewhat higher than Council homes, but there is obviously no shortage of people able and ready to take up any vacancies.

And so we come to the end of Bray's "Main Street." It is not too difficult to picture it some four hundred years ago. "The Crown" as cottages, Shottery and Stuart Cottage, Jones's, The Old Dutch House – all connected with the working of land in one form or another; a rough road leading straight from today's Windsor Road to the lychgate and church, built over tree-trunks laid transversely, and increasing over the years in height above the floor-level of the cottages; the rows of cottages on Church Lane; Chauntry House (then small) beyond; the old cottages on Church Drive; the rooms over the lychgate possibly housing the parish priest. All forming the nucleus of what was to become a busy and happy village.

UPPER BRAY ROAD

Crossing Bray Bridge, beside Jesus Hospital there are open fields on each side and a fine batch of assorted trees beside the pavement. One needs to see them on the way into the village to enjoy them fully, but we will walk on now, until we meet the first house, AVALON. Built about 1920 it was originally four small rooms. Now two have been combined to make one large sitting-room, and in 1960 the modern kitchen, bathroom, and study were added. Next is KILNDOWN, built in 1952, was named by its owners after the village in Kent whence they came, and has no reference to Mr. Murray's kiln at Court Cottage.

LANDELAY was built in 1954 on land which had been the meadow of BRAMERTON, which stands on rising land above the road. Taken over in 1959 by Berkshire County Council, it was previously a lively if noisy place with vociferous kennels. It was built in 1930 by Mr. Jones, the builder, for himself.

Now for the two roads off Upper Bray Road. We see here HASTING CLOSE, a cul-de-sac of nine houses built in 1961. Eleven years of growth, trees and shrubs are the only alteration to the original scene.

Not so the other road, CANNON HILL CLOSE. Though only recently named (and inaccurately spelt!) it was originally the property of a Mr. Saunders. In 1914 he moved from Braydene, in Ferry Rd, to the CANON HILL BUNGALOW at the far end of the present road. A gate at the entrance to the drive bore a replica of the notice he had had at Braydene. It read, "No hawkers. No circulars. No sky-pilots." In Ferry Rd its predecessor had been tarred and feathered, and whoever had been responsible for the incident lost no time in repeating it at the new site. Thereafter it was known locally as "Tar-and-feather lane." The unfortunate Mr. Saunders had not only found the village unco-operative with his attitudes (he was nicknamed "the Mayor of Bray") but he had also fallen out with the Vicar – hence the wording of the notices. (It may be worth mentioning here that he was no relation to Mr. Saunders of Weir Bank Farm, a generation later.) He sold the bungalow in 1918 to Mrs. Westcott, who subsequently sold it to Mrs. Hoult in 1949. She describes it as being well-built, with hand-made doors and window-frames and originally being lit with gas-lamps.

The next to arrive were 3 black wooden huts. These had been transported from Holyport, where they had housed German prisoners-of-war. One on the left is called Hillside, while opposite it are two called "The Retreat" and "Treesbank", which was previously "The View." In spite of their unhappy origins they have formed welcome homes until now, when plans are in hand for their replacement by modern buildings. In 1968 came three modern houses, TUDOR ROSE, GABLES and CAMBERS, while what appears to be the last available space in the road is supplying another house, at present un-named.

Now cross the road and see COURT COTTAGE and OLD COURT COTTAGE. Old Court Cottage – tucked in beside the M.4, this used to be the gardener's cottage to Bray Court, (the derelict red brick Victorian house between the Windsor Rd and the M.4) and stood in the kitchen-garden, with a vinery, out-houses and stables near by. (The M.4 gobbled up the stables.) Originally it was only two-up-two-down, plus a small kitchen. The bath-and-toilet used to be beside the present front door, but in 1958 it was re-sited on the upstairs landing.

The kitchen had an old lead pump for the water, now removed except for its unusually decorated handle. This is now fixed into the wall, as a decorative feature.

In 1925 the whole Bray Court estate was offered for sale, in lots. The purchasers of the cottage, outbuildings and land westwards to Upper Bray Rd and south to Windsor Rd was a famous potter named William Staite Murray. A true artist, it was he who re-instated pottery as a fine art as opposed to a craft. He came to live here in 1927, installing a potter's wheel in one outhouse and a kiln for firing. He was Head of the pottery section of the London School of Art, and had a one-man exhibition in London every year. Many beautiful examples of his work are in the Metropolitan Museum in New York, in Toronto, and in the Victoria and Albert Museum in London. He named every piece, which was a new departure in the history of the art. The titles summed up the "mood" of the pot, to which form, colour, movement and surface all contributed. As a rule the forms were simple but extremely subtle, and the glazes generally in grey, buff, olive or brown. He also held one-man shows in Paris, The Hague, New York and Tokyo.

He stayed in Bray until 1939, during which time he had

transformed the vinery into a studio, beautifully furnished, where Art School students came for the day and which became a magnet for many artists and sculptors – among them Henry Moore and Barbara Hepworth – and which even now brings art students from schools and colleges to see where he lived and worked, his kiln and his wheel. An interesting feature of the kiln was that it incorporated a new idea of Mr. Murray's. By using oil instead of wood for fuel, and by placing two heaters opposite each other to concentrate the heat, it was possible to raise the temperature of the kiln to a far higher degree than had previously been possible.

A master-builder from Grantham was so impressed that he asked to be allowed the privilege of building it himself.

In 1930 he added to the west end a house for his mother-in-law, which now constitutes COURT COTTAGE, which is the only part of the buildings visible from the road, and is still occupied by a member of the Murray family.

A recent attempt to develop the whole estate with modern houses was unsuccessful for practical reasons, but one might hope that the world of the Arts would consider it worth while to safeguard a place of such pioneering success and interest.

FERRY ROAD

In the 18th century it was called Thames Street. If we stand at the bus-stop we are on land once known as "Holmans Mat." At one time it was a grassy plot overshadowed by a great tree. There was sometimes a mini-fair held here, with a tinkers stall; games both here and in the orchard opposite; and general merrymaking.

Came the 20th century and came Mr. T.J. Digby, and all changed. He bought the orchard, which stretched from Braydene to the High St. He bought the two cottages beside the Ringers Inn, and demolished them. The Mat was reduced to its present size in order to widen the road.

He hired builders at 4d an hour and a foreman at 6d an hour, and produced, in 1904, the row of houses, FERRY END.

But first, the war memorial which was dedicated to the fallen of the 1914–18 war by the Bishop of Oxford, in 1920. A stone with the names of casualties of the '39–'45 war lies in front of it. The rose-beds were a gift from the Women's Institute.

Now, Ferry End – what tales these cottages could tell! Certainly some, and probably all at varying times, have earned their local nickname of "Mustard Row." The original lessees (at £24 p.a.) would not have given their official addresses as being in Bray, and the occupants would have had many shared experiences of a 'dramatic' nature! A decade later several were 'clubs.' A licence to sell liquor was all that was required. Bridge and gaming-tables, and congenial company provided the amusements.

Together with the Tan House, the George Inn and the Hotel de Paris they contributed to the teasing query by non-residents, "Are you married, or do you live in Bray?"

Structurally they were never identical, internally their one common feature being the living-room entered by the front-door with a stair-case leading out of it to the bedrooms above. Today alterations have been made mostly at ground-level, providing small but modern kitchens, either incorporated in the original building or as extensions, and providing homes for citizens highly respected and respectable! They were all sold by Mr. Digby in 1923 as the rentals no longer paid for their upkeep, and they have been individually owned ever since then.

In the sale catalogue of 1923 they are advertised as:–

"Nos. 1,2,3,9 and 10 – 4 bedrooms, 2 reception.

Nos. 4,5,6,7,8 – 3 bedrooms, 1 recep. Electric light, water and gas laid on in each house.

Nos. 11 and 12 have been converted into one. 6 bedrooms, 2 bathrooms. Lounge hall. Very large lounge. Sitting-room, Dining-room. Full-size Billiard-room. Brick-built garage for 2 cars."

The final half of these is NEEDHAM LODGE, at one time the "Isis Club," when there were many gay evenings in the large room at the back. It was also the home of relatives of the famous aviators, the Warwick Wright brothers. The story goes of their landing their plane in the field opposite Braybank; sending for the police to guard it all night; visiting their relatives at Needham Lodge, and returning next morning to fly off. This caused great excitement among the villagers, who flocked round, prams and all, to see it. It is said that the wind caused by the propellers sent skirts billowing over heads – "and we didn't wear tights in those days, either!"

The garage to this house now has a flat over it, but it used to house a pony and trap.

Down a long drive we come to CANNON LODGE. This, too, used to be coach-house and stables, whose owner lived at "Thames Villas" until 1914 (c.f. Braydene End). In 1957 two architects took it over, creating a pleasing home within the structure. The top floor used to be the hay-loft which contained a boarded-off corner where the stable-boy slept. This has been retained as a "built-in" cupboard.

The name of the house has nothing to do with Cannon (or Canon) Hill. The father of one of the architects had once built a large cannon, and they had a model of it in the house. Confusing in this area, but now recorded for posterity!

Now back to the road, we find BRAYDENE and BRAYDENE END. These semi-detached houses were, in 1898, one house built by Mr. "Tot" Saunders. He had pulled down a previous pair, semi-detached, known as "Thames Villas" which appear on OS maps of 1871 and 1875. Within the grounds there were good-sized coach-houses and stables which were retained unaltered (now Cannon Lodge).

The groom lived there too, for we have a record of two sons being born there, in 1899 and 1902.

Several interesting features remain at BRAYDENE END.

Beside its front door, which used to be the back door, there is a hole in the wall. An ex-garden-boy relates how he had to bring a cow every day to be milked. It was tethered to an iron ring in the wall (still there today), milked, and the milk then weighed, (not measured), on a spring-balance attached beside the door. His first job each morning was to pump water from some 14-foot-depth under the sub-soil to fill the tanks in the large greenhouse. The pipe for the pump can still be seen behind some bushes.

Within the house there remains the mosaic tile flooring in the hall. This was laid by Italian workmen specially brought to do the job. They lodged in The Terrace, and could speak no English, so returned home as quickly as possible!

A large room at the back must have been a still-room, for it has an iron hanging-rail across it, for keeping meats etc.

Near to it was a capacious wine-cellar (but at ground level) amply fitted for its purpose.

The present owner has put a new ceiling in the kitchen, 2 feet lower than the original.

Mr. Saunders was evidently one of the "characters" of Bray in his day. Memories describe him as being short but upright of carriage, "just like King Edward," dressed in Norfolk jacket and knee-breeches, and a trilby hat with the fashionable "shaving-brush" adornment on its back. He carried a big stick (which any lazy employee would feel the weight of) and was accompanied by a very large Airedale dog. Others remember him with a chuckle, as "Mayor of Bray – or thought he was" but he was always ready to help others and did it efficiently too. On one point all agree – his swearing. This upset some parents, who kept their children away from such a bad influence, and even his male contemporaries found it a bit much. One wonders whether the Vicar, the Rev. Raymond or his successor the Rev. Riddlesdell, remonstrated with him. Anyway, he fell out with one of them for he had a notice put on his gate "No hawkers. No circulars. No sky-pilots." This was tarred-and-feathered by some local joker at dead o' night.

A considerable timber-merchant, his business was ruined by the first world war which stopped his imports from Russia. He moved to a small bungalow (in which he incorporated his remaining good timbers) during the war, and sold Braydene (see Canon Hill Close).

The Colliers were the next owners, still using the whole house – as it stayed until 1939, when it was divided into three flats to house evacuees from London.

In 1956 it was re-designed as two houses, there today.

Braydene End was bought by its present owners in 1968, but "One Braydene" has had but one owner since 1956.

Up another long drive now to FOUR SEASONS. In 1963 the land for this house and garden was sold by the owners of Vicarage Cottage who no longer wanted such a large garden.

The house is of modern design, with large picture-windows looking onto a long lawn. This land has to be kept open by Church decree, as the Vicarage overlooks it. A welcome open space in a rapidly-filling village.

Next to it is VICARAGE COTTAGE. Probably 14th or 15th century, it was originally two cottages for foresters of Windsor Forest, of which Bray formed a part in those days.

Facing it, the left-hand cottage was the smaller, just one-up-one-down. The other had two-down plus a byre, and two rooms above. In the ceiling of the present sitting-room one can just distinguish the place where there was a "coffin hole." This used to be needed because the staircase would not permit of transporting a coffin, so it was let down through the hole.

The actual chimney served a fireplace in each cottage and is still essential to keep the house upright.

The floors used to be 2 feet below street level, and would have been of earth covered with straw. Unlike the other old cottages in High St., this would always have been above flood-level. Naturally, it has a new board-floor now.

One front door faced Ferry Rd, the other was at the back.

It used to be half-timbered with wattle-and-daub all over, but 50 years ago the side facing the path to the church fell out and was replaced with plaster-rendering. The front of the house, too, was covered over at that date.

In 1852 the church bought it with money from the sale of some land to the Great Western Railway. It is referred to in the Rev. Austen Leigh's memoranda Mss as "the orchard and cottage east of the church-yard." It was then vested in the Bishop of Oxford.

The present owners had rented it for seven years until 1959 when they sought to buy it.

There were no title-deeds, so the Bishop required that they procure two sworn affidavits from two of the oldest inhabitants to the effect that "they had always known it to be Church property". Hereafter any future owners will stand possessed of title-deeds to their property – after centuries.

In the garden is a chestnut tree over 100 years old, and five fine limes, which add considerably to the attractive surroundings both for the owners and their neighbours.

Any ghosts? Yes, one of the White Lady genre. She was a frequent visitor until a few years ago, but being of a happy disposition she caused no difficulties to anyone.

The cottage is a Grade II "listed building."

Across the church lane (created by the Rev. Austen Leigh) we come to what used to be one large house, THE OLD TAN HOUSE. Was it a tannery or wasn't it? Nobody knew but all supposed it was. Then I chanced on a reference to a "Tann-Howse" on the river, which appeared to be between Maidenhead and Windsor, though no location was specified. I badly needed to claim it for Bray, but in all fairness to Windsor had to give them the chance to refuse me. However, their searches could uncover no reference to a tannery – which puzzled them as much as it pleased me! Somehow they had never noticed their lack of one. But I hereby claim it until such time as a prior right is firmly established.

Supplementary evidence was produced by the account of an ex-gardener to the house who said "Yes – he'd turned up a great many animals' bones and skulls when he was digging there, long before all these alterations of course."

There is also the curious feature of what appear to be brick-lined arches of, possibly, drains, which were revealed during the construction of the bungalow lying parallel and nearer the river. Captain Turk, of Cookham, says these could originally have been wood-lined, and bricked at a later date.

Remembering that Bray used to be part of Windsor Forest, and the King's demesne, it would have been useful to transport the hides of hunted animals by water, for their transformation into materials for boots, gloves, jerkins etc, etc.

The house, of course, is centuries later. Again I can find no firm date. But it does appear in a painting of the riverside at this point – signed and dated 1883. Three families are remembered between 1897 and 1930 – viz, Cooper-Smith, Adlam and Lamplough.

Then came years of gay parties given by its new owner, Fayette Perry. A well-known stage beauty herself, many other famous names were included among the guests.

Memory records that she would put away the silver chandeliers, and set the candles on the table in empty champagne bottles. From dinner to dawn the wine flowed, laughter and song held sway, and the hostess would sometimes contribute to the gaiety by dancing on the table.

The following morning, the gardener always brought a bucket into which he emptied the remaining champagne from glasses and bottles. This he would dilute with water and feed his tomato-plants with it. The result? The finest tomatoes in the parish!

These parties continued until 1939, when Hitler successfully blacked-out both houses and gaiety. Soon, she had Canadian soldiers billeted in her house.

A warm-hearted and generous person she always gave a party at Christmas for the "old folk" of the village, giving them presents in money or in kind to take home when they left.

She left in 1947, and died in America. A small headstone in the churchyard bears witness to her sojourn here.

Thereafter the house was run as a hotel and night-club by two different owners, for nine years.

Came 1956 and came Mr, Pick, a builder. He saw a house with 6 bedrooms; a library with a parquet floor, facing south; a dining-room where 22 people could dine in comfort; a drawing-room overlooking the river; kitchen quarters running the full length of the side facing the Vicarage; and two bathrooms. The gateway was surrounded by a wrought-iron arch bearing the name "The Old Tan House," and there were garages to its left. In the garden, beside the river, was a ballroom with old beams, and parquet flooring throughout.

With remarkable alacrity he transformed the whole collection into four dwellings. THE OLD TAN HOUSE was made from the drawing room, hall, and bedrooms above. NEW TAN HOUSE from some of the south-facing rooms.

TANHOME became a bungalow, from the ballroom. TANSY COTTAGE utilised the garages, and TANNERS was partly old and partly a new addition, bounded by a high brick wall built to contain it apart from The Old Tan House drive.

So passed the last of Bray's famous – or infamous, if you prefer it – record of some thirty years of "joy unconfined", as experienced in its private houses.

At the gates of the gay house there is RIVER COTTAGE. This is joined to the Waterside Inn, but has never been part of it. When it was modernised recently the stripping of paint from the sitting-room door revealed the words "Coffee Room" on the room side of it. This led to the supposition of its having been part of the inn, but is quite unsubstantiated. At this time also the removal of floorboards in the sitting-room uncovered a well some 15 feet deep, and half full of water. An old grave-stone was on top, which was immediately replaced and the well made watertight as far as the room was concerned, before replacing the floor. Unfortunately nobody thought to make a note of the name on the stone. Alterations consisted of modernising the kitchen and making one room out of the dining and sitting rooms.

Now we come to the WATERSIDE INN. Like the legendary Vicar of Bray it has changed coats several times. In the 19th century (and maybe earlier) it was called "Charlese," a private house but providing teas and mineral waters when requested. The surroundings were rustic. It stood at the junction of Thames Street (Ferry Rd) and a pathway beside the river which turned at right-angles through the then Vicarage kitchen-garden.

There were bushes and trees where the boat-house now stands, and the road was rough and unsurfaced. Its history as an inn is recorded in another chapter. Between its two inn-lives the house reverted to its name of "Charlese" and was owned by Sir James Baird.

The boat-yard's history belongs to the river section. From here we can walk back on the south side where there is a row of small cottages. The first three are appropriately called FERRYSIDE and are, at present, owned by the family of the late G. Messum. Beside them are WATERSIDE COTTAGES, three more of apparently the same vintage. An accurate date is not known but they are probably pre-18th century. The gardens at the back were known locally as "King Charles's rubbish dump", but they may not date back so far. These are numbered 2, 3, and 4. Number 1 has now been incorporated into LINUM COTTAGE which has far more appearance of being 18th century. This was the original Waterside Inn (recorded elsewhere) but has been a private house for many years. Next to it is ROSE COTTAGE which is a century older – real "olde worlde." The famous book "Tom Brown's Schooldays" was written here, by Thomas Hughes. It probably opened straight onto the road originally, and acquired its front garden later. In 1923 this was full of rose trees, and the front wall of the house was covered with climbing roses. There were cast-iron railings atop the brick road-wall. A photograph of it appears in the sale-prospectus of 1923 but unfortunately is not suitable for reproduction here. In it, the end wall is shown weather-boarded, and a large chestnut tree is beside it. This refutes one report that it had always been joined to JASMINE COTTAGE, on the corner of Bettoney Vere. In 1923 it did not exist, but at some later date rooms from Rose Cottage had the present corner-section added, the whole being made into one separate abode. The sitting-room, stairs, and room above are the later part, while the old beams, nooks, and crannies bear witness to their belonging to a much earlier century.

This site is unoccupied in a map of 1875. Indeed, the land from there right up to the garden of the Old Dutch House is, at that date, HILL HOUSE, a farm named for its owner, Mr. Hill. Probably 18th century it has no deeds dated prior to 1923. The house is said to have been similar to the Albion Inn. A central front door flanked each side by small "parlours", with bedrooms above, it may have been the farm-owner's house, but in the late 19th century it housed the farm-manager for Mr. Eggleton, who owned both the Mill and Hillhouse Farm – a considerable acreage. Two handsome old barns behind the house still remain, but the house itself has been considerably extended and modernised in the past 20 years.

Perhaps this is the place to report on: –

BETTONEY VERE

This is a row of six houses built in 1906 by Mr. T. J. Digby. The land had previously been an orchard. On it stood a large barn which he removed to the end of the lane beside The Terrace, and here "Granny Hale," from Church Lane, had pegged-out her laundry-lines to dry and freshen her customers' linen.

The houses were rented until 1923, when so much of the property in Bray went under the auctioneer's hammer. The row had its quota of "clubs" during the hectic years, but later quietened down with the rest.

A brief flash of publicity in 1967 came with the discovery at No. 2 of a painting which had been "lost" to collectors and art-historians. This was recognised by Mr. David Carrit, of Christies, London when visiting Lady Joan Baird's house.

It was a small painting, only 18¾ ins by 14½ ins hanging above her fireplace. He knew it to be a portrait entitled "St. Ivo" by the great Flemish master Rogier der Weyden. It had disappeared in the Middle Ages and re-appeared briefly in the 19th century. Its fortuitous discovery here caused great excitement in all art circles, and eventually the National Gallery bought it from Lady Baird's executors in 1971, and have now put it on show to the public.

THE TERRACE

On the early maps this was an orchard owned by Mrs. Trenchard.

By the end of the 19th century it had passed into the ownership of Mr. Woodhouse who built the present houses.

They are in 3 sections. The first to be built was the centre block. An astute use of materials readily and cheaply available enabled him to provide good homes at little cost. Gravel dredged up from the river contributed to the building of the walls; most of the woodwork – panels, thresholds, and windows – came from the very hard wood which had formed the wooden bridge across the Cut by Jesus Hospital. Much of this remains in use today. This block had the address of "New Cottages" until the terrace was completed. It is now composed of Nos 7–12.

The second section was on the road end. No. 1 was built as a butcher's shop, and the block completed by 1899.

The next year the far end went up, in concrete. The chimneys were made from drain-pipes lowered into place and then surrounded with concrete – somewhat predictably they always needed frequent sweeping!

Beyond these were the remainder of the fruit trees, an area which formed a communal drying ground.

At the far end are garages. Before Bettoney Vere was built this was the large barn on its site. Mr. Digby had it removed to its present position where it has formed much-needed garages for about 60 years.

The allotments were originally rented from The Fishmongers Company and extended to the roadway, as the Village Hall was not built until 1924. The land now belongs to the Clothworkers Company to whom the Council pay rent. An increase in the number of plots available is expected soon.

A small area just beyond the present plots, and adjoining the land of the Village Hall will, before long, be landscaped to improve the whole scene – thanks to the generous terms of the Clothworkers Company, in permitting and assisting the development.

And so to what is referred to in early accounts as "the corner shop." This started life as a butcher's shop, Poultons, in 1899, and had trouble with the road-drainage between it and "the new road" (Brayfield Rd) in 1910, a familiar difficulty recurring up to recent times. Later A.T. Sealey became a competitor to the Jones family in groceries, at one time taking on the sub-post office from the current Mr. Jones, who had found that forty years of the "privilege" was as much as he wanted.

In 1935 Mr. Bowler, father of the present owner, purchased the business, post-office and all. November 5 was the opening date, well remembered by his sons because there was a Guy Fawkes bonfire on the allotments which got out of hand, and both boys were told to go and put it out.

After the war they learned the business, eventually taking over from their father in 1958. So far it had been a small affair – just a counter, a very small "box" for the post-office, and storage space behind. The family, pre-war, had a small sitting-room downstairs with a window over-looking the lane, and bedrooms above.

Now things started to move. Mr. Sid Gay made the alterations necessary for doubling the selling-space by taking in the whole of the ground floor. A number of more exotic items were stocked towards the back of the shop (which Stanley always managed to sell to at least one husband I know of!) and business continued to expand. This necessitated a further extension in 1959.

All these years deliveries had been made by van, but the difficulties of labour and of van-maintenance were proving uneconomical here as elsewhere, and in 1963, having bought the adjoining house, the decision was taken to change to "self-service." Further alterations were made and in 1966 there were rumblings and grumblings by the customers at the new way of life. These turned to wails of despair the following year when the Bowlers left the village to the tender mercies of Budgen's. Perhaps many of us had not fully realised until the family left how much they, singly and collectively over two generations, had contributed to our comfort. For three years the larger firm kept going, but Bray did not really enjoy the experience – shopping was done as a routine chore, the life had gone out of it.

Many of the "regulars" were thankful to find sanctuary with the Jones family, who also re-assumed the burden of the post office. Then one day the news broke – the Bowlers were coming back! Newcomers to the village wondered what all the excitement was about but soon learned the difference it made to have Stan and Elsie smiling and chatting and helping. Their family business is very "young" compared to the Jones's but during the 36 years it has become very much part and parcel of the village's life.

As to the bricks and mortar, opinions vary over the decor externally, in a village setting. The interior is modern and well planned for traffic-flow from door to goods to pay desk to exit. The floor above is now a self-contained flat owned and let by the Bowlers, but not inhabited by them.

BRAYFIELD ROAD

The Homestead was the first building to be built here, by T.J. Digby, to house some of his employees at Weir Bank. There was no road, just a rough gravel track.

From the corner facing Bettoney Vere to the Albion, and taking in all of Brayfield Road houses and gardens, was Hill House Farm. Here stood two old railway carriages used for storing cattle and chicken food. Their doors still had "2nd Class" in gold and black lettering but the roofs were thatched against the weather. Huge ricks of hay and straw stood around, and there was great excitement when the threshing-machine was in action. The corn was then taken to the Mill, producing an excellent and fine flour.

There were also sheep-pens which were moved daily to provide fresh fodder which was specially grown for them.

Mr. Eggleton owned both the farm and the mill in 1910, but when he died his son decided to sell-up, and emigrated to Canada.

Mr. T.J. Digby was the purchaser. Having already built Ferry End and Bettoney Vere he saw the possibility of building here too.

In 1911 his first venture was "New Cottage" now called FAR END "If that will sell, opposite the pub with all its hustle and bustle, then others can be built," he said.

It sold to a Major Lee and remained unaltered until 1960, when the present owner Mr. Robins, added the drawing room. BRIAR COTTAGE was the next to be built in 1912, and let to Mr. Allsopp, who bought it in 1914 for occupation by his wife during the war-years. In 1928 it became the property of Mr. E. Howes who still lives there today.

There soon followed BRAYFIELD COTTAGE let to Mr Roland Cock in 1923.

WHITE COTTAGE, let to R. Coward in 1923.

DOVEMEAD, previously called Dovercourt, let in 1923 to Captain Berkley MP.

CLEEVE, previously called Degresley, let to L.E. Lacey in 1923.

CARELESS CORNER. It was so called in 1937 by Mr. Greenhill because so many visitors leaving the Hotel de Paris took the wrong turning at that point! In 1923 it was let to L.J. Lumsden, and it was once owned by Mrs. Gulbenkian.

Of these, Dovemead was rented until 1960 by Mr. Shirtliff, and was called Dovercourt until present owner, Mr. Abraham bought and re-named it. Mr. Shirtliff then moved next door to White Cottage.

CLEEVE was originally a small two-up-two-down cottage.

On the opposite side we have PEN-Y-BRYN built in 1964 in part of the garden of Picket Post, for Mr. Vivian.

BARNACLE LODGE, originally called CRANNOCK, is a bungalow now owned by Commander Kennard, who is having a bathroom and bedroom added this year.

Turning the corner towards our starting point, we first find THE HAVEN another charming bungalow built 1925–27. From 1948–69 Mr. and Mrs. Stamp lived there. They were closely concerned with Biggs of Maidenhead, the famous shop in Maidenhead High Street, renowned for their expertise in antique furniture and much patronised by Royalty.

ALDWYCK LODGE was built in 1928–29. This is the original part of the building. Aldwyck Cottage was added in 1961–62 as a house for the owner's mother, Mrs. Gilbert Scott, who had previously been living at Brook Cottage on the opposite side of the road.

That takes us across, where we see:

BROOK COTTAGE,

CHESTNUT COTTAGE and

SOUTHERNWOOD.

These appear to have arrived in the 1923–24 period. One presumes that although they had been envisaged as following on the East-West section, the first World War intervened and the development had to await the availability of labour. The chestnut trees were planted in 1924.

Before leaving this area we ought perhaps to return to the previous section, since there used to be a house on the corner, behind Bowlers, called "The Little House." This stood on land marked in the Bray Inclosure Award map as being owned in 1819 by the Bishop of Oxford. In the early 1900's there was a small house wherein lived Mr. Sable, with coach house and stables. He hired out a horse-drawn cab, a precursor to today's taxi-hire.

It was subsequently greatly enlarged until it looked anything but a Little House compared to its neighbours.

About 1960 the whole site was bought by a builder who submitted plans for five houses. In spite of emphatic opposition by many local people he obtained permission, and by 1964 we had:

BRAY CLOSE

Nos. 1-5 were built first, followed a year later by Nos. 6 and 7. These last were built in the shrubbery of The Little House. Their new owners, in constructing their gardens had to dispose of numerous empty gin and whiskey bottles!

At number 5 lives Mr. Frank Bough, a sports commentator on BBC TV.

At number 7 lives Mr. K. Dudley who has served on the Village Hall Committee and the Bray Preservation Society. It was he who, in 1969, successfully persuaded so many people to plant daffodils in gardens and hedgerows, creating a gay atmosphere in the following spring.

OLD MILL LANE

Originally known as Arbour Lane in 1871 and later as Monkey Island Lane for the full length from The Terrace to Builders Wells corner at Windsor Road, it was re-named when the M4 was built and the fly-over bridge constructed.

It includes the road running north from it to the old mill. East of the fly-over it is still Monkey Island Lane.

The first section from the Village Hall, has no houses fronting it, but across the Brayfield Road intersection the long story begins.

"On your left you see" HILLHOUSE COTTAGES, Nos. 1 and 2. These date back, probably, to the 18th century when they were the homes of labourers for Hillhouse Farm. With outside walls a full 18 inches thick they were well constructed.

In 1923, they were for sale by auction and were said to be "let on weekly tenancies amounting to £29. 9s. 11d. per annum."

No. 2 has been modernised inside, but No. 1 has some interesting features of which the most attractive are the two bedroom fireplaces. They have small "hanging grates" built some 9–12 inches from the floor into brick side supports. The chimneys being straight, the draught is direct, and the wood fires, though small, give a good heat.

Additions to the house comprise a small dining-area to the sitting-room, and a "glass-house" studio at the back of the kitchen where the artist-owner, L. Dench, can give rein to his talent. Examples of his work are owned by many people, and pubs, around the Maidenhead and Windsor area.

THE HERITAGE. In the sale of properties of 1923 only the land was sold, and that only by an "abstract of title." This persisted in regard to the land adjoining Thames Cottage (land later used for a tennis court) until 1952 when Dr. Harris bought it outright. The house was built by Mr. Smale in 1925, who sold it the following year to the Misses

Bennett and Cocks.

Dr. and Mrs. J.E.G. Harris lived here from 1952–1970. He served on the Parish Council and Cookham RDC for many years, winning the respect and affection of the village for his constant concern for its welfare.

The present owners have added a play-room extension on the ground-floor.

THAMES COTTAGE. Built before 1914, it is for sale in 1923 "of modern construction with large garden in front. Let at £91. 5s. per annum." The garden extends at the back to Brayfield Rd where there is a brick-built garage.

MARYLAND. Built soon after Thames Cottage, and slightly smaller, nevertheless it had a tennis court and outbuildings in its large garden which extended as far as "Far End" on the corner of Brayfield Rd. VIRGINIA now occupies a part of the garden.

Built in 1964 on the opposite corner is TWO WAYS COTTAGE. Originally there was a fine old barn with 16th century beams where cows were brought to be milked. In 1793 a small one-up-one-down cottage was added. Then Mr. Crispe built the large house on the river behind it, which he called "Two Ways," and with it he took over the barn and cottage. This he divided into a garage with a room above for the chauffeur (which is now the large sitting-room, new stairway and room above). The other end provided accommodation for two sisters who were the laundry-maids of whom one washed and the other did the ironing. To this has since been added a modern kitchen.

In 1942 it joined the happy band of "clubs" – with tennis and bridge being specified – but not for long.

Before starting down this long lane we should turn up what was once a private drive. Here are two houses, MERRYDOWN and BRUNGERLY, built respectively in 1967 and 1969. Beneath them was the en-tout-cas tennis court mentioned above, so the land-drainage is excellent. The drive leads on to CHARMIAN and WYTCH HOUSE which were once "Two Ways". Before it was built there used to be an inlet from the river running at an angle to the Albion Inn. This was filled in during 1920.

The world-famous architect Baillie Scott designed the house which contained six bedrooms and five attics above a large dining-room, oak panelled; a lounge; and a very fine entertaining-room with a curved ceiling and a minstrels gallery. The floors are all of solid oak and the timbers for the doors and beams are all reputed to be 200 years old. They were divided into two dwellings in 1952, each house having a part of the dining-room but WYTCH HOUSE has the other large rooms. The minstrels gallery area has been incorporated into a bedroom above the main room. In 1972 the two houses were declared to be 'listed buildings.' There is a new hard tennis court in the garden.

Beside it, on the river-bank, approached by a narrow tree-lined lane, a modern house is nearing completion. It replaces a bungalow called "Bray Bungalow."

Back to the lane, and we find APPLE TREE COTTAGE, built in 1960. The history of The Albion Inn next door is dealt with in another chapter.

Now comes BRAYBANK, a large development of flats and houses built in 1964 on the site of the famous Hotel de Paris. To be honest, its arrival caused great consternation, disapproval and distress, but, equally honestly, it was partly the village's own fault for being so apathetic about local government and planning. At first by no means attractive, in spite of some of the old trees being retained, it has since been well landscaped and is less of a builder's cuckoo in a village nest.

Next to it is an open field belonging to HOME VIEW. This is a very old property. In the 18th or early 19th century it is said there was a paper-mill here, and subsequently a foundry (one old map of 1871 bears the words "site of foundry.") The engine was housed in a hut beside the house and "made a terrible noise." There was a very tall chimney on the house in the paper-mill era.

All the land from here to the Ferry was owned by two

generations of Mickleys who operated the wharf from the mid-19th century. One of the daughters married a Mr. Lamb of Marylebone, London. He took over the house for the use of his family during the summers, having the theory that country living was "better than doctors" and that his children could get enough schooling during the winter months! At that time there was only a ladder providing access to the bedrooms, and the only water available was from a well outside the kitchen door, drawn up in buckets. About 1900 Mr. Lamb added the present square bay windows and the back kitchen over the well, which is now covered by a large stone slab.

Beyond the fence there used to be an orchard. (Yet another one! Bray must have been a good sight in the spring, and full of vitamins the rest of the year!) The present owners had to remove many fruit trees in order to build CHELMERS, in 1959 from part of the land of PADDOCK COTTAGE, built about 1932 and still in its original shape. TREONA, DORMTIKI, and LOWRIES were all built about 1925, with the subsequent insertion of RECESS, about 1930. Here we turn in to:

RIVER GARDENS

When the old Mill was in operation this was part of its land. There is a report, but no record, of a windmill here. It was sold to the Newcombe Estates about 1920 who proceeded to build upon it. One of the residents today describes it thus:

> "A peaceful spot bounded on the North by the Thames and on the South by Old Mill Lane, and sufficiently far from the M4 to permit a restful night's sleep. Four acres of meadow separate the houses which now completely surround it. Since the construction of the river bye-pass (the Cut) the Thames, though often restive, has been content with its banks; the last flood was in 1961 and covered the whole area. Access to the

river is provided for the residents. A private road serves each house in the quadrilateral, and ramps are maintained to discourage those who might be inclined to regard it as a race-track."

The building had started in 1921–22 when BANDOL, BALQUHIDDER, and BRAYMILL COTTAGE were completed and sold.

In 1922 Newcombe Estates held a large sale entitled BRAY MILL ESTATE with illustrated pamphlets of suggested designs of houses and plans of sites.

"The plots have generous depths, varying from 140–200 feet. The Company will be pleased to submit plans and Estimates for the erection of Houses and Bungalows to suit the requirements of prospective purchasers."

The sale was held in Braywick Court Hotel, later to become the Hotel de Paris.

HIGH TREES was built in 1926. Double-fronted with a large garden with river frontage and a tennis court, it was the home of the film star Diana Dors in the late '50s. In her fast, smart boat she gave much pleasure to the riparian owners between Bray and Maidenhead on summer evenings.

On this (left hand) side of the square the last house to arrive was TRANQUIL, built in 1964, and has had only one owner to date.

Houses with river frontage are: STEPPING STONES, a bungalow with a large garden. One report is that there have been several dwellings built and pulled down and replaced, starting in 1926, making it difficult to date the present one.

There is a strip of land giving access to the river "for residents only" between this property and BRAY WILLOWS, a large house and garden which was built in 1940. This land would have taken in several of the sites on the original plan as would also WILLOW BANK, which is different in design. It was built by Mr. S. Gay in 1935–36. BRAY VILLA, a smaller property was built in 1959.

WEIR HATCH, another larger house also built in 1959, is the last on the river bank.

Turning back, inland, there are now seven houses of which the oldest is MOLLEN built about 1946, but with additions and alterations of recent years; and HERONS GATE, THE CONIFERS, BARLEY END, KARINA, and THE LINDENS all built in 1963. Starting life as bungalows, several are having additional rooms this year. HONEY HOUSE was the first to be completed. Mr. Macdonald Hobley, well known on TV and radio, lived here.

PIPERS END facing north was built 1954–55. A "granny extension" is being added this year.

Back to Old Mill Lane:

BRAIMEL, arrived in 1925, and was extended in 1928. It is named for its bee-keeping and honey.

Why there was a lull in development is not known, but BRAMBLES was not built until 1937.

Then, of course, the Second World War dominated the scene and the fields remained open and "full of beautiful poppies" until 1956 when SHERBROOK, and TROON, appeared. The following year the decrepit labourers' cottages on the next corner were pulled down and replaced with OAKLEY and CHOLA GHAR.

And that's the end of houses facing onto Old Mill Lane.

The lane leading north to the Old Mill has the same postal address today but was at one time called Mill Drive (a reversion to which might help postmen today and tomorrow).

The first house on the right, RED CEDARS, was built in 1958. This was the first "open plan" house in Bray with its large L-shaped lounge, kitchen and three double bedrooms above. MILSTED was a year earlier, 1957.

DADANAWA did not appear until 1968. The unusual name stems from the owner's connection with Guyana. Two years later, 1970, saw lorries full of building materials plying up and down the lane where once "you could tell the time exactly by the farm-cart which took the grain to the Mill. It was the only traffic here then."

CAPRICE, GRAYSLEY, MILL LODGE and MILLSTONE were the end-product of all the activity and were quickly inhabited.

The end house on this row is nearly finished (1972). It has had a chequered career. Originally meant to be built, within and without, of exotic and expensive materials, it was never fully completed. Some eight years later building was resumed more realistically but fire gutted much of it. Today it seems nearer completion, but has no name to record.

BRAY MILL

Without doubt the oldest building in the village. Kerry quotes from documents that "Bray Mill and Manor were given in 1206 to Jordan de London by King John . . . confirmed in 1218 by Henry III at the yearly rental of 12 shillings." For centuries the millers owned and controlled their weirs, exacting payment for adjustment of the waters in the passage of craft. This was a constant annoyance to watermen everywhere, and Bray mill owners were convicted of "taking excessive toll" in 1370, 1451 and 1489. Thacker names Thos. Ward as the owner in 1633, and Mr. Lewis in 1843.

Mr. Eggleton owned it in 1909, together with all the land now occupied by River Gardens, and the fields from the Mill to the Old Mill Lane. He also owned Hill House Farm which included today's Brayfield Road.

On his death all his property passed to his son who, however, had other ideas. He decided to emigrate to Canda, and sold his inheritance to Mr. T.J. Digby in 1910–11.

The mill continued in action until the wheel was removed in 1915. Mr. Digby lived in The Mill House from 1916–1923. (A year which might well be dubbed "The

Year of the Great Sale", since it affected the village so much!) The blurb in the auctioneers' catalogue is extensive and of sufficient interest to bear quoting.

> "Original Bray Mill and The Mill House, now made into one residence of moderate size – wonderful old oak beams have been preserved. One beam, supporting the roof of the Billiard and adjoining room, is 60 feet in length. The present owner had the Old Mill Wheel removed, in order to make room for a turbine to generate an electric current, but the war intervening, he adopted the alternative scheme of a motor with accumulators, which are in perfect order and produce current at about 1d per unit."
>
> Accommodation comprised:- "Inner and Outer Halls. Dining Room, Morning Room and Drawing Room. 11 Bedrooms. 4 Bathrooms. Billiard Room, with room leading from it 34 ft by 31 ft over the old Mill Wheel."
>
> There are "grounds of 5–6 acres, with hundreds of 10 year-old fruit trees, a Hard Tennis Court with Summer House, two lawns to the Mill Stream and one shady and restful lawn on the Main River below the Weir."

Greenhouses, potting sheds, a garage for two cars nearer Old Mill Lane, and staff cottages with corrugated iron roofs complete this portion of the estate. I have not found a record of the purchaser, but it is known that the large house was divided into its present two dwellings at that time.

Memories relate that Mrs. Pease, in the Old Mill grew wonderful vegetables due, she said, to "never planting anything except when there is a full moon." She left in 1945, and was followed by a famous ophthalmic surgeon, Mr. Romano.

The staff used to live in OLD MILL COTTAGE adjoining, where there were two bedrooms, kitchen and living-room. It was bought in 1955 by the present owner who added the large glass-walled room in 1960. A keen and skilful gardener, he has turned the orginal plain paddock into a beautiful garden, rich with colours all the year.

Two of the old mill-wheels are now in the garden.

The final acres of Old Mill Lane are at present not built upon. There is a large barn near the river built by Sir Hugo Cunliffe-Owen as a piggery but never used as such. It is to be removed this year (1973) and re-erected on Weir Bank Farm which owns this inverted L-shaped area of land. It has river frontage forming one area, and the other running parallel with the motorway and emerging at Old Mill Lane where the fly-over bridge begins. The remaining rectangle of land has been used for horticulture but recently has been left fallow. Its future is uncertain.

Before leaving the lane we must notice the other side of the road. From Brayfield Road to the motorway are open fields, all arable, owned by Weir Bank Farm. They are bordered on the roadside by a very fine line of trees, mostly horse-chestnut, which provide much beauty to the area, particularly in Spring, and which are protected by the imposition of a Tree Preservation Order for the benefit of the public.

And so to the bridge. From its centre we can look back over the Lane we have left, with its variety of architecture, its early history at The Mill, its most recent additions in close proximity, its English scene of fields, trees and populace – the best vantage point locally to recognise that Bray is a village, in modern terms, though our forebears called it Bray Town.

MONKEY ISLAND LANE

From this point on the bridge as far as Windsor Rd is Monkey Island Lane. The earliest ordnance survey map of 1871, shows it as Arbour Lane with but two houses opposite Monkey Island. One on the river bank called Brayfield Lodge (not Long White Cloud), the other abutting on the lane, named as The Hut. This poses problems as we will see later. The whole of the rest of the land was farmland until 1905 when the indefatigable T.J. Digby built for himself WEIR BANK, a large house with a long river-frontage, and an imposing drive from the lane. It contained many rooms and a very fine staircase with carved panelling beside its entire length which was reputed to have "cost more than the whole of the rest of the building", possibly an exaggeration, but it was certainly a fine feature. An unfortunate fire in 1972 destroyed it.

The name cannot have applied to the main weir, which is upstream at the Mill, but there may have been one of the numerous fish-weirs nearby.

He built at the same time a cottage beside the house for the head-gardener; the two farm cottages in the fields opposite; and the lodge at the gates of the drive. This is now a private house called WEIR BANK LODGE. For a few years it was divided into two flats, but in 1970 it was re-converted. The present owners created one good kitchen from the small rooms, added a garage, and re-positioned the front door. Opposite the drive is AVONDALE, built in 1921. The head groom lived there in Sir Hugh Cunliffe Owen's time, and it now houses the farm-manager. We are now on:

WEIR BANK FARM. It was bought, along with Weir Bank House, from Mr. Digby in 1921 by Sir Hugo Cunliffe Owen and used principally as a Stud Farm. In those days it extended westward to Upper Bray Rd, southwest to Windsor Rd, and north to Brayfield Rd. It was self-supporting as to the stud, and had other arable produce as well. Sir Hugo bred 25–30 horses, of whom the most famous was Felstead, the Derby winner of 1928. An account of the local celebrations of that event will be found in "Bray Village Hall," a truly memorable occasion. Sir Hugo and his wife were great benefactors to the village, still being spoken of today with much respect and affection. He and his wife remained at Weir Bank until 1932 when Mr. Oppenheimer bought it, but the Stud Farm was retained by Sir Hugo until 1946, during which time he had a further success with Rockfell, sired by Felstead, who won the Oaks in 1938.

In the same year the government compulsorily purchased the land needed for the future main road to the west, (later to be the M4). Fences were set up which effectively divided the farmlands, and foundations were laid for the bridge over the Thames. The Second World War intervened; the road-building lapsed; and the farm continued.

In 1946 Mr. Saunders bought it from Sir Hugo and increased the stud to as many as 76 horses in 1954. Thereafter numbers declined. A herd of Jersey cows was maintained until 1971 when the farm, already reduced in size and divided by the M4, was returned to arable, and a pig-farm substituted for the horses. There are today 133.4 acres of which 30 acres around the home-farm will be permanent pasture.

The two small cottages which used to house the farm-labourers are now converted for the owner and her family.

The last house on this side of the lane, before the Cut, THORNEYCROFT was built early this century, and has remained unaltered structurally.

Not so the opposite side which has seen much activity in the last 20 years.

The first to catch the eye is TEMPLE COTTAGE, facing the lane. This is one of the puzzlements on the 1871 map. It is clearly marked and named "The Hut", which presupposes one house only, but until very recently there were obviously two semi-detached labourers' cottages, of Georgian period. Moreover, "The Hut" was the name of the house now called "Long White Cloud," by the bridge, in late Victorian times. One is tempted to suppose that the cartographer surveyed this area after too long a visit to 'Monkey Hall Hotel' (as he records it) or even settled for filling in his befuddled memories the next day!

The evidence for Temple Cottage originally being 2 cottages lies in its chimneys, and its 2 staircases which would have been superfluous in one relatively small house. It is currently being extended on the north side, nearer the corner of the narrow lane leading to the river.

Before the bridge to the island was installed, in 1956, it was necessary to ring a bell and wait for someone to row a boat over to fetch you. But today you walk over a metal sided wood-plank bridge to reach the beautiful lawn shaded by huge walnut trees. Here a stone-paved path leads you to:

MONKEY ISLAND HOTEL

This is one building where we can be sure of beginning at the beginning, thanks to A.L. Rowse. In his book "The Later Churchills" (published by Macmillan, London and Basingstoke) he quotes a letter from Lady Hertford in 1738 describing the island Charles Spencer has bought.

"He has a small house upon it, whose outside represents a farm, the inside what you please; for the parlour, which is the only room in it except a kitchen, is painted upon the ceiling in grotesque, with monkeys, fishing, shooting etc and its sides are hung with paper. When a person sits in this room he cannot see the water, though the island is not above a stone's cast over: nor is he prevented from this by shade; for, except for six or eight walnut trees and a few orange trees in tubs, there is not a leaf upon the island; it arises entirely from the river running very much below its banks. There is another building which I think is called a temple . . . It should seem that his Grace has taken a hint from the Man of Ross's public spirit; and in order not to copy him too slavishly, has bestowed a treat upon the eyes instead of the bellies of the passengers," (up and down the Thames).

The whole appearance and accommodation of both buildings have been considerably altered in the past decade.

In 1963 the dining-area was increased by the addition of a large glass-sided building on the landward side, which enclosed a tree, with a fish-pool at its base. Music and dancing were then possible.

In 1970 a further room was built at the upstream end. It extended the full width of the building, and had walls handsomely decorated with battle-scenes appropriate to its name, "The Marlborough Room."

The Temple, too is quite changed. Its first additions were rooms to make it a private dwelling, but in 1970 further rooms were added to form 30 bedrooms for hotel guests. The buildings are listed Grade I today.

Accurate accounts now depend on local memories. A description of the temple tells of its having no ordinary rooms, as such – on entering, one went to a staircase which curved up to a banquetting room with windows giving a fine view up and down the river and across the fields. The ceiling was beautifully painted pale blue, with clouds and cupids and ribbon streamers. The whole edifice was octagonal, and stood somewhat higher than the Hotel.

Mrs. Plummer ran the hotel about 1908. She was noted for her excellent cooking which she would serve in the dining-room which had been added at the back of the Monkey room, also on the lawn in Summer, where cast-iron tables and chairs were provided. Drinks were served through the window of the bar beside the Monkey room. There had also been added upstairs rooms to accommodate the family of parents and five children.

There was, early in this century, a monkey kept chained to one of the walnut trees. Called Jacko, large brown and hairy, he sometimes escaped and found his way into the village. One of his escapades had tragic consequences.

A pregnant woman, near her time, returned to her home in The Terrace to find Jacko seated on her kitchen table munching chicken bones. Scared, she ran up the row to a friend's house, tripped over the step, and fell heavily. Her son was born prematurely, but stillborn. The distraught father swore he would wring the neck of any monkey he saw in future.

Access to the hotel had to be by water. Several punts were kept for ferrying coal, wood, stores etc and two with cushions for visitors. On the landward side was a grassy slope, but a half-dozen stone steps had to be climbed to reach the lawn on the island. When there was no telephone all post and messages were delivered by hand. It was no light matter to travel the lane. In bad weather the mud was a foot deep, and in summer the ruts and ridges made equally hard going for carriages, traps and vans. A narrow footpath, marked out by white posts, made life more bearable for pedestrians. Not until Sir Hugo Cunliffe Owen's arrival was it re-made to a better surface, and the tarmac laid much later.

In 1962 the hotel's menu-covers propounded the theory that the monks of Burnham had owned the island, and therefore it had been "Monk's Eyot." Research has proved that there were no monks, only canonesses, at Burnham, certainly since 1266 A.D. Nor have they ever owned any land up-river from Boveney. So, for origins of the name we are back to the decorator of the "small house upon it." The artist, de Clermont, was known to have a fetish about monkeys and was probably given carte blanche as to choice of subject.

There is a tale, which I have been unable to confirm, that George III in his sad, mad days lived on the island and had a monkey as a pet.

Now let's return to see the houses between the river and the lane. (Don't worry – the bridge really does sway a bit. It's not that last gin!)

Now – the first house of the row is LONG WHITE CLOUD. The building is probably 150 years old. The back is constructed with old solid timbers, some 15 inches thick, and old bricks. The front portion and the chimneys are mock Tudor, and were added in 1896. The front door of RIVER COURT was the door of the whole long building. The lounge at the river-end was added later.

Originally, it included RIVER COURT and SUNDIAL

COTTAGE. It was named by a New Zealand owner, that being the Maori name for his country. Before that it was called "The Hut." Its last owner under that name was Mr. Frank Schuster who went there in 1911. He was intensely musical, consorting with famous musicians. Two famous singers are remembered locally. Clara Butt, whose powerful voice reputedly could be heard outside the Albert Hall when she gave recitals; and Nellie Melba for whose training he paid. The latter sang at the opening of the Village Hall. In the grounds of his house there was a large wooden building with a stage, known as the Music Room. It had two large bay windows to the main room; a kitchen; and living quarters for staff. Thus it remained until 1959. Here he would entertain his friends and arrange concerts by ambitious and able young musicians hoping to win recognition in their profession.

Memory also relates his friendship with Sir Edward Elgar who composed some of his music in "the room in the shape of a cross" where he would use the grand piano.

A 20-foot-high fence of iron uprights and railway sleepers surrounded the garden in those days, ensuring privacy for all these famous people.

Before Mr. Schuster, one of the owners was Miss Van de Weyre, in 1893. She was a lady-in-waiting to Queen Victoria, and one local memory relates how the Queen, when at Windsor, would send a telegram announcing her intention of an immediate visit. This arrived at the Post Office (Mr. Jones' shop) whence a runner was sent off post-haste to The Hut lest Her Majesty should arrive unannounced. Presumably The Hut was one place where she *was* amused?

Later, the racing-driver Stirling Moss lived there. Mr. and Mrs. Saunders, of Weir Bank Farm often spent weekends with the family and eventually bought it from them. Five years later they sold it, and it was then divided into three dwellings.

THE MUSIC ROOM, a modern house, (standing on the site of the old building), was built in 1963 as was BROOK HOUSE.

AUGHTON COTTAGE used to be the coach-house and stables, with a flat above for the groom and his wife. The living accommodation is still upstairs as it was considered to be a flood-risk at the time, the new Cut not then being in operation. This was in 1961.

On the ground floor one can still identify the original uses. There remain some of the square blue-stone bricks; the garage shows in its old bricks the corner of the coach-house; the hall once stabled two horses, the troughs in two corners being boxed-in today; likewise the "utility room" behind it. A staircase was installed, but the original access to the living-quarters was an outside ladder. The accommodation comprised a living-room, and bedroom, plus a hay-loft. This last was made into a bedroom by dropping the floor and entrance by 18 inches. The living-room was increased by an addition beyond the beams, and a bath-room added. In 1968 more accommodation was provided on the riverside by the addition of an attractive passage leading to a new bedroom originally standing in the grounds of The Hut. "The groom's cottage" now has a 66 foot river-frontage to its garden and an historic and comfortable conversion to modernity.

Bounded on one side by the lane, and on the north by the original high brick wall one can visualise what a delightful "estate" it used to be, with trees, shrubs, flowers, and lawn sloping to the rivers. A quiet backwater with music and musicians delighting all and offending none, though one does wonder how far Clara Butt could be heard!

The lane was tarmaced when the fly-over was made, but from Temple Cottage onwards it is still rough, rutted and pot-holed as far as the Cut. This was done on purpose, to discourage traffic from the south.

Over the Cut, on the left is BRAY MARINA, constructed in 1965 for the mooring of 300 private boats. It was formed from the open water left by gravel extraction and enabled The Thames Conservancy to insist on the clearing of a conglomeration of houseboats etc. which had progressively littered the river banks. The Marina is provided with a chandlery, petrol services and a provisions shop and a large carpark, and caters mainly for week-enders and holiday-makers.

With gravel extractors working each side of the lane and their lorries churning up the mud, the whole scene was one of desolation for years. However, plans are afoot now for leisure pursuits, boating, fishing etc., on the reclaimed land to the east and the lake on the west, with a properly surfaced road serving them, which should improve the lot of the long-suffering residents from Monkey Island to the Windsor Road.

Of the houses on the west of the road, the first to be built was QUEENS EYOT COTTAGE, in 1928. Here lives the warden of Queen's Eyot, the island opposite the Marina, which belongs to Eton College.

POMONA FARM dates from 1939. Its orchards of apples and pears also provided sites for some half-dozen caravan dwellers until 1973.

Six more small houses arose between 1948 and 1959 ending with CLERICUS HOTEL on the corner.

This is the area referred to in the account of the Chauntry and the Church as BUILDERS WELL and BUILDERS CROSS. Mr. Michael Bailey translates this into Saxon BEILI DUWIES CROES, meaning "the courtyard of the Goddess of the tumulus (of death?)", and "the water place" of the same goddess, which ties up with the fact of a spring and the legend of the Saxon church.

GAS LANE

Perhaps few people today realise the origin of this lane.

It is so called because there was once a gas-holder there. It was a do-it-yourself project by the then owner of Canon Hill House to provide his own gas. Up to 1970 it was possible to see its foundations, which were circular, of about 15 feet in diameter, and it is remembered as having "a hexagonal lid, with a long metal arm over it."

The foundations are now earthed-over in the land adjoining BARNWELL COTTAGE, owned today by Mr. Donovan, but built by Mr. Sawford for Mr. Higwell. Under the hall there is a well, also safely covered.

On the right, going up the lane is SYL RICH, built in 1970 and named for two members of the family, SYLvia and RICHard. Mrs. Rolls moved there from MANSFORD HOUSE, next door, built in 1939 also by Mr. Sawford. All this land had been part of the grounds of Canon Hill House.

Within the next large gates is GRANGE COTTAGE. This was converted from old outbuildings of Canon Hill House in the early 1930's by F.C. Pollard of Taplow. In 1972, during excavations, for the addition of two rooms, an old yellow brick wall was revealed. This had been part of a 20 foot square enclosure for a dung-heap!

The long building beside this house is said to date from Charles II and was retained by Mr. Pollard after selling the big house and land.

One wonders how, and if, this links up with a report that the Causeway used to be known as King Charles' Causeway, used by him to ride dry-shod to the Crown Inn; that the foundations of Braywick Cottage appear to date from that time; the gardens at the back of Waterside cottages were called King Charles' rubbish dump; and he is widely reported as visiting Nell Gwynn at the other end of the Parish.

Turning north, and uphill, we find on the left KNOWL HOUSE, built in 1969 in the garden of what was then called "Walnuts", now THE OLD HOUSE. This started as the cottage for the head-gardener of Canon Hill House in the 19th century. In 1969 Mr. Pollard enlarged and modernised it, and sold it to its present owner, Mr. R. Crawley. Next to it are four semi-detached cottages, WOODBINE COTTAGES which also housed employees on the estate. Now privately owned they are small, originally two-up-two-down, but have added extensions at the back of recent years, and they are still happy homes with their own small gardens back and front.

Next to them are the offices and yard of R.S. Winter, Builders, and then HIBBERTS, both of which Mr. Winter built in 1957.

On the opposite side is WYCKEMEADE owned and built in 1960 by Mr. J. Dean and ADELAIDE HOUSE built in 1971 in the garden of Braywick Cottage.

All of this lane is un-made, which helps to retain the rusticity it has always enjoyed.

HIBBERT ROAD

From Gas Lane we look across to an open landscaped area with beautiful old trees. Not so long ago, in 1969, we saw only a high brick wall. This enclosed the property called BRAYWICK LODGE which had been there since the 18th century, owned in the 19th century by the Hibbert family who were great benefactors to this parish.

The gate, set in a semi-circular brick wall, still stands, but most of the house was demolished in 1968–69. Look left, and see CORBRA COTTAGE. It was built in 1958, replacing five old cottages on that corner. They included a bakery and a tuck-shop facing Hibbert Rd; and three houses for employees of Braywick Lodge facing the main road. Outside Baker Allens shop on the corner was a large "bumping stone". When there was a "beating the bounds" expedition the ladies of the company would be "bumped" on this stone, which rocked on an uneven base. The memory of this still causes a chuckle locally, but a refusal to elaborate any further.

Now, turning right, we first find BRAYWICK COTTAGE. It is thought that this was formed from two cottages of considerable age. Its foundations appear to be of the Tudor period. It has very thick walls and old oak beams. The present height and extent of the rooms, and its more recent brick facing suggest re-building in the 18th and 19th centuries.

The pleasant garden, which included a tennis court, has recently been "developed" for three new dwellings.

THE COACH HOUSE was built in 1971 where the previous coach house/garage stood.

The last plot is today awaiting a further house.

The land from here to the Causeway was once the kitchen-garden to Canon Hill House. In 1937 it was owned by F.C. Pollard, who proceeded to build on it. The first house was WELL HOUSE. Previously there was a five-bar gate used for delivery of coal, wood, etc. Also a brick archway leading to the well. The present archway is of the original bricks. This well was used for storing ice. Enquiries have elicited that the ice was probably manufactured at Slough whence it would have been brought on horse-drawn open carts, the ice-blocks covered with sacking, and huge "tongs" provided for handling them.

2596. *The Excavation for the ice-well* where the situation is either of a dry, chalky, gravelly, or sandy kind, may be made entirely below the surface of the ground; but in strong loamy, clayey, or moist ground, it will be better to raise the well so high above the surface, as that there may be no danger from the wetness of the soil.

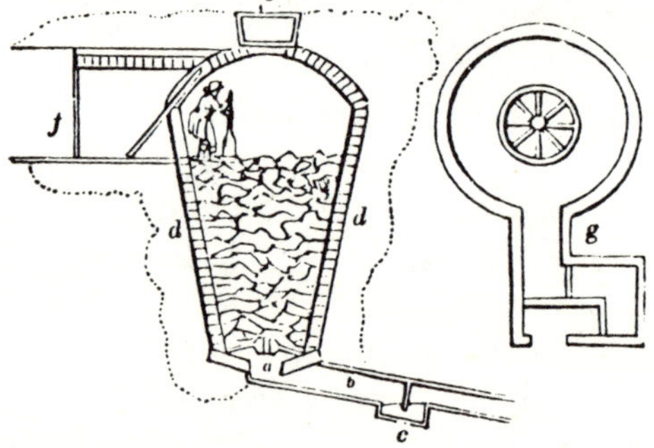

2597. *In building the ice-well* there should be a space about two feet deep left at the bottom (fig. 618 *a*), for receiving any moisture which may drain from the ice; and a small underground drain (*b*), containing a stop or trap for the exclusion of air (*c*), should be laid from this, to carry off the wet. Over the space at bottom (*a*) should be placed a strong grate of wood or an old cart-wheel, to let the moisture fall through, which may at any time be produced by the melting of the ice. The sides of the well (*d*) must be walled up with brick or stone at least two feet thick; or the wall may be built hollow. When the proper height is attained, the wall may be arched over with two arches with a vacuity between, leaving in the centre a hole for the admission of the ice (*e*), and in the sides a door for taking it out (*f*). This door, in order the better to exclude the air, should open into a porch (*g*) with the three other doors, the spaces between which should be filled with straw to exclude more effectually the heat of the atmosphere. The doors should not be on hinges, but be made in two or three parts, falling in a rebate, or groove, from the top; this makes the removal of the straw in the porch unnecessary, when taking out supplies. The whole being covered first with a layer of tempered clay and next with a hill of earth, the appearance will not be disagreeable (fig. 619), and may be made ornamental.

Ice House

2598. *Management.* When the house is finished, it should have time to dry before the ice is put into it; as when the walls are moist, the damp of them frequently dissolves the ice. At the bottom of the well, upon the wooden grate, some small faggots should be laid; and if upon these a layer of reeds be placed smooth for the ice to rest upon, it will be better than straw, which is commonly used. In the choice of the ice, the

> thinner it is, the better it may be broken to powder; as the smaller it is broken, the better it will unite when put into the well. In putting it in, it should be rammed close, and a space left between it and the wall of the well, by straw being placed for the purpose, so as to give passage to any moisture that may be collected by the dissolving of the ice on the top or otherwise. If snow be used instead of ice, it ought to be pressed very firmly together, so as to exclude air, and in fact approach in texture to ice. To aid in consolidating both ice and snow, a little water may be occasionally poured over it from the rose of a watering-pot. An experienced gardener, in filling his ice-house, after laying down the ice outside the door, pounds it into particles not larger than those of sand or salt. He then carries it into the house, and throws it into the ice-well, in which a man is placed with a rammer to beat and ram it closely; occasionally sprinkling it with a little water to consolidate the whole. When this water is impregnated with salt at the rate of 10 lbs. to 10 gallons, and poured on the ice in such quantities as to saturate it completely, the ice will become as firm as rock, and will keep three times as long as when common water is used. It will also be found to keep much longer when exposed to the air. The reason is to be found in the well-known chemical fact, that salt water, and consequently salted ice, has a less capacity for heat than fresh water or fresh ice. (*Ency. of Cott. Arch.*, § 737.)

The beams within the house were made from boat-timbers.

For its first 35 years it was owned by the Chamberlain family.

The following year, 1938 saw the construction of NEW HOUSE and CAUSEWAY END. Mr. George Harding of Hope Cottage remembers all this building going on; the builders digging down over six feet, seeking gravel for the footings but finding none, whereupon he allowed them to take it from his garden which was only a few feet away, at only one-spit's depth; the squirrels sitting on the kitchen-garden wall brazenly eating and enjoying peaches taken from the trees on the other side.

Before going across to his cottage we will just look at the last house here: WILDACRES. This was originally called "Up Yonder", and was built by F.H. Jones for his own occupation from 1958 until 1966, when it was bought and renamed by Mr. Peter Simpson, a solicitor in Windsor. Set in a large garden with a spinney at the end, he tamed some of the wildness and has now sold the whole property to the developers of the Canon Hill House estate, but first carefully placing restrictions on encroachment, demolition of trees etc.

The flat over the garage has been used as a "Granny flat", i.e. to accommodate a relative of the owner.

The rough lane, the waterfall and the Causeway all provide a relaxing, happy atmosphere at this point.

Now across to the line of old cottages which face up Hibbert Road. At HOPE COTTAGE we can hear Mr. George Harding's account of them,

"Originally there were only the three middle cottages here, and I was once told they were 16th century. Anyway, I know the two end ones were added later, for I had to knock out the fireplace-wall once, and found an obvious doorway-opening. And the other end of the row there's wattle-and-daub walls before the final cottage. Anyway, this doorway of mine had been filled in with boards, sacking and wallpapers, and it took four barrow-loads of bricks to make it good. At one time this cottage was for an estate-worker at Mr. Hibbert's house. His wife must have done the laundry for them. There's an outhouse at the back which had a big copper in it, and a steam-pipe leading out through the wall. Inside, the back room has a sky-light which provided light for the ironing-table. (A thoughtful gesture by the generous Hibberts?)

"From the back garden you can see the alterations made to PEAR TREE COTTAGE next door. The big windows were put in, for enjoying the view over the fields, by Miss Henniker-Heaton. It was sad she died before she could live in it. HAZELCOT next to that looks much the same as it always did. Then ROSE COTTAGE my end and GREENWAYS, earlier called Ivy Cottage, the other, were added in 1870 and they were owned by the Hibberts, too. The stream across the bottom of our gardens is dry now. The new Cut did that.

"I don't think I can help you much with Bray, you see, I was always a Braywick man.

"Different villages? Yes. Look here. That's a photograph of the Braywick tug-o'-war team. That's me, there. We had matches against the Bray team. Always different villages, we were. I worked for Sir James Clark, at Braywick Grove (now Braywick House). I was the estate carpenter's mate. All sorts of jobs I did, including sweeping the chimneys. But that's outside your area for the book, isn't it?"

Much later, 1962–64, Mrs. Kempton lived at Greenways where she found some Roman coins in the garden, which she gave to the Reitlinger Museum in Maidenhead.

Going on down the hill we come to an area marked on an old map as "OSIERS" – fields of them. ("Heer bee bogges" again!).

We find two semi-detached houses, one of which, originally called "Blarney Cottage," is now called RED EYOT. This is probably a corruption of Rod Eyot. This field was called Little Eyot, and that one opposite, across the road, was Big Eyot and both were known as Rod Eyots, as they supplied osiers and willow-wands (or rods) for making baskets and furniture in High Wycombe.

This house and HALCYON COTTAGE were built high to minimise the effect of frequent flooding which was always a problem until the new Cut was made. Even in the early 1900's all the fields around here were referred to as the eyots (or Aits) which probably implied there were some firmer patches of land among the water and reeds.

The date of the houses is not known, but on a map of 1870 there is a suggestion, no more, that houses might have been there. It is known they existed before 1914.

Both cottages were built and owned by Col. and Miss Campbell, "Halcyon" being still in the possession of a descendant. Additions to the rear of the original buildings were built in the early years of this century.

The next house is a recent arrival. BROOK HILL was built in 1967 by Mr. B.A. Zwannenburg. There had previously been a small wooden house and garden, with a notice board offering "Teas", but trade cannot have been very brisk.

The heavy rains in 1970 again accumulated around the house but drained away within a few hours.

Whether or not this occurrence affected the judgement of the Cookham RDC is a matter for conjecture, but the adjoining plot of land was deemed "subject to flooding" when its owner, Mr. Peter Watts, applied for permission to build a house on it alongside TRAVELLER'S JOY, a caravan home of many years' standing.

Turning in at the next gate we really do get above flood-level, for this house is at the top of a steep drive. Called BRAY BROC, the "Broc" is probably from the Old English word 'brōc', meaning a small stream or marsh, either of which would be applicable here.

It was built in 1898 by Blomfield, for Mr. West Neve. Now divided into two dwellings the part nearest the road was formed from the stables and coach-house. If future owners or archaeologists were to dig in the garden they might be puzzled to find complete foundations for another house. The answer is simple. The then owner of Bray Broc planned to build a cottage there but his Bank manager and creditors were too strong for him! The whole site was filled in and covered, forming the raised garden to be seen today.

And that's the end of the houses in this road. The school and its surroundings are recorded elsewhere.

The remaining fields on this side were cleared of all their pollarded willows in the latter part of the last century in order to produce more land for pasture. With the draining of the land there disappeared, alas, a colourful display of kingcups, wild iris, and meadowsweet. The gypsies, too, were upset for they had always robbed the willowsticks to make the clothes pegs which they hawked around the neighbourhood!

WINDSOR ROAD

For the purposes of this book we are staying on the village-side of the road. It makes a neat package of the area under examination.

Starting then, at the corner of Hibbert Road our first house is called THE ELDERS. Thought to have been built some 150 years ago, it may have been formed from two of the three cottages built for and used by the staff for Braywick House (formerly Braywick Grove). There used to be a building behind it which could have been a coach-house.

The present name is not botanical, but related to the sculptured stone figures beside the drive, said to be elders of the Scottish Kirk.

It has recently (1971) been enlarged at the south end, giving a large and light modern lounge with an open staircase to the new bedrooms above.

At the back of the building are a range of single-storey rooms built in 1961.

The cottage in the front, previously called Ashley Cottage, is being re-built today, to form office accommodation for the business in progress at The Elders.

Next door is "The Stag and Hounds," reported in another chapter.

Now we come to: SAWFORD'S GARAGE, a new building set back from the main traffic, with its own slip-road. It started life in 1921 as a small service and repair shop beside the erstwhile "Hare and Hounds" pub opposite Hibbert Rd. In 1930 the business moved to the present side, but nearer the "Stag and Hounds". With the building of the Braywick roundabout the present re-location was both necessary and advantageous, for owners and customers alike.

Behind and beside it is THE LODGE to Canon Hill House, which was built for the head-gardener and his wife in more expansive times. In its garden is the old hexagonal dairy with a double roof for air circulation, and tiled interior. It must have been a very attractive feature of the estate, with the trees around contributing to the shade, and the stream running nearby.

By the time this is being read, the big house will probably be no more. Bulldozers will have eliminated for ever the rectorial manor, and some twenty-eight or more houses will be rising from the ashes.

Nevertheless, since Kerry gives it scant attention, this seems the time and place to record some of its inhabitants and its development, as a salute to its existence.

But first, perhaps this is where there should be settled the present uncertainty as to the spelling of "Canon". There is no proof whatever of there having been any cannon in this area, not even a concealed ack-ack gun in the '39–'45 war, whereas there is ample evidence that it was of ecclesiastical origin.

The whole of this area formed part of the Manor of Bray and was the rectorial estate of the Canons of Cirencester.

Probably from Saxon and certainly from Norman times the estate of Manor was held by the King who put it into the hands of whomever he would should manage its affairs, both spiritual and temporal.

An early 17th century "Terrier" (i.e. survey of property) in Salisbury refers to the parsonage 'we have the house commonly called the Canon house' whereas one of a mere 50 years later gives a detailed description of the vicarage by the river (i.e. 1677–1954). This seems to indicate a rectorial property in the Canon Hill area, though no exact site is specified.

CANON HILL HOUSE

The origins of a house here are hard to find. To quote Kerry:

> "The rectory was appropriated to the Abbey of St. Mary, Cirencester, between 1293 and 1301."

This applied to all the lands until 1547, when Edward VI granted them to John King, Bishop of Oxford, and his successors. In 1608 Sir John Norris held "the parsonage of Bray" as tenant of the Bishop. No house is mentioned, as such.

In May 1650 a survey "for appointing the sale of Bpp's lands for the use of the Commonwealth etc" does provide evidence of a building.

"A fair Rectory or Parsonage House, being a new brick house with outhousing, yards, and gardens enclosed with a brick wall, containing about 2 acres of land. It has fields adjoining in Holyport field near the said Parsonage house, containing in all about 50 acres . . . and 10 acres of meadow . . . and a meadow called Wickmeade." This gives the picture of a large house with fields stretching to Upper Bray Rd (Holyport field) and to Hibbert Rd (Wickmeade.)

Sir Henry Master is the lessee from the Bishop.

The reference to a new brick house could mean "as opposed to a previous house," but no evidence has been produced so far.

In the same document is the report that the vicar, Hezekiah Woodward "hath a vicarage house," i.e. a vicarage then existed in 1650. The location is not specified but in 1677 the present "Tudor House" (q.v.) was already the vicarage, so it may well have been the Rev. Woodward's home in 1650.

To digress for a moment, one Roger Noke is said to have a small copyhold on the Canon Hill lands. Could he have been the Noke of "Nokes Hole?" (see chap: "Home from School".)

Kerry leaves the "brick house" at 1650 and the search begins for subsequent occupiers. The next date turns up in 1732, when Lady Coleraine lives there, and gives Bray its first, and only, fire-engine in 1737. Ascanius Williams, who died in 1780 is also connected with it. Either Lady Coleraine or Mr. Williams employed the famous Adams brothers to design and build an addition to the house about

1750. The porch with its typical Adam decoration above it; the rainwater-heads bearing the date 1750; the ceilings and mouldings; the doors with their furnishings; and the handsome fireplaces, all bore their imprint.

Canon Hill House – circa 1935

Next, Lyson refers to it thus "Canon Hill, the feat of James Law Esq is the rectorial manor, together with the advowson of the vicarage, held on leafe by him under the fee of Oxford." He must have left it to his wife, for in the Inclosure Award it is mapped as belonging to Mrs. (Elizabeth) Law. Kerry joins in again when he writes,

"This estate having been enfranchised by the representatives of the late Mrs. Law was purchased in 1857 by J.H. Palmer Esq of Fulham. It is now (i.e. 1861) the property and residence of his son, Edward Howley Palmer."

The private chapel referred to by Kerry was, at some time between 1861–1900, turned into a billiard room. Its table was still there in 1933, an early type made before there were cues, the "weapons" being then usable with complete decorum by ladies as well as men!

An afternoon spent peering at old gravestones in Bray churchyard produced, inter alia, the fact that Sir Richard Malins "late Vice-Chancellor" died a few days after his wife, Susannah, in 1881. He being "of Canon Hill." The Dictionary of National Biography relates that he was Knighted in 1867; fell from his horse, 1879; became paralysed, was made member of the Privy Council, and retired – all in 1881 – and died the same year, his wife's death having accelerated his own. He left no family. No mention is made in this report of his living in Bray, though his burial is so recorded.

The Adams family (no relation to the architects) were in the house from 1893–1909. It was during this time that the gasometer was installed in the grounds (now Gas Lane, q.v.) for home-produced fuel.

It was then sold to Edward Stanley Dawson, passing at his death to Lady Elizabeth Dawson, Lady-in-waiting to Queen Mary, subsequently to her daughter, who married Lord Bingham in 1929, and sold the house, its gardens and half the hill to F.C. Pollard in 1933. The other half was bought by G.N. Smale. In this deed F.C. Pollard undertakes that the houses he shall build shall be "not more than three detached dwelling houses to the acre" and that they shall cost "not less than £1,000 each with outbuildings and garage." Also, that they shall not be for any trade or business.

The map attached to this Pollard/Smale purchase shows "The Hollies" and "Bix House" already *in situ*, but no other buildings anywhere on the estate which extended from Hibbert Road to Upper Bray Road.

In 1934–35 Mr. Pollard sells the house and its grounds only, to H.F.S. Morgan.

He converted the ex-chapel, billiard-room and one beside it into kitchen-quarters to make life easier for his staff by putting them at ground level instead of in the previous semi-basement. Some of his staff remember, today, their happy life with the Morgans.

During the war Mond-Nickel took over the house as offices.

Later it was bought by Berkshire County Council for an old people's home. It remained thus until, in the late '60's, a fire gutted the roof. Mercifully nobody was hurt, but the old folk were removed; the house left to predatory vandals; and the whole estate sold in 1972 to a developer. There is permission to build 28 houses and a road.

So passes Bray's oldest Manor. One cannot but regret the loss. The house, though not one of England's beauties, stood in erstwhile lovely gardens overlooking open fields towards the village. It is the last, as it was probably the first, notable building of Bray Town. Its occupants, both masters and men, led busy and happy lives by no means isolated from the rest of the neighbourhood.

Many of the handsome trees are bound to disappear though one hopes that some will be reprieved, at least near the stream which has run for so long through the grounds and out at the "tumbling bay" into what was ungraciously termed in 1819 "Public Drain No. 1," that is, the Cut.

One interesting item should be recorded. From 1622 until very recent years all who owned property on the Manor (i.e. Canon Hill House and the new houses in Canon Hill Drive) undertook to subscribe to the repairs of the chancel of Bray Church, thus maintaining the old link between matters temporal and spiritual extending over some 650 years.

It may seem pointless to record the history of a house probably vanished from view by the time this is in print, but the documents are at present scattered, and it may be of some use to historians, and of interest to some who have known it, to have them here set down.

Back to Windsor Road, and almost at once we find, leading off is

CANON HILL DRIVE

The whole of this hill used to be the woodland park of Canon Hill House.

After F.C. Pollard bought the whole property from Mr. Morgan (in 1933) he started developing the hill, completing the 7 houses in this road by 1938. All are well constructed and of a good size, with gardens which are large by today's standards.

The first house to be built was OAKWOOD, in which some fine old timbers are incorporated and the front door's carving is from oak on the estate Mr. Morgan moved into this house, from the manor house, obtaining permission for a pathway connecting it with the old estate and its lodge, where his head-gardener lived. Its present owner is Chairman of the Bray Preservation Society and also serves on the Bray Parish Council.

FALCONHURST holds a potential surprise in its garden for any future digger-upper, viz: an old bricked-up air-raid shelter from the '39–'45 war.

HEATHFIELD. Built in 1930 it was first called 'Chestnuts' as it has a sweet-chestnut tree reputedly 170 years old. It then became 'Littlefield'.

LITTLE LUNCES is thought to refer to fox-holes. It was built in 1938.

WHITE GABLES reduced the size of its garden in 1971 by selling a part to accommodate a new house.

The remaining houses at this time are WHITEOAKS, ELMSTEAD, and THE BRANT.

CANON HILL WAY

Building by G.H. Smale here started in 1933 with CANON HILL COTTAGE, shortly followed by CHERRY TREES, WHITE COTTAGE, ST. CHRISTOPHERS LODGE and LONGRIDGE.

In 1957 part of the garden of White Cottage was sold and

THE ORCHARD, aptly named, arrived. THRUSHES was built in 1936 of old bricks and timbers which added to its appearance of "genuine" age. Its very large garden was also reduced by sale to provide OAK HOUSE, in 1960.

The land a-top the hill remained open fields until 1963–65 when it was developed with six houses.

WAKEHURST, FAIRFIELD, IONA, HIGHFIELDS, APPLEDORE, and TIMBERSCOMBE.

At the bottom corner is THE CEDARS, which with TANGLIN and BIX HOUSE were all built by F.C. Pollard.

OAK TREE HOUSE has its date, 1935, visible and was built by a builder in Windsor. It is well-named, not only for its surroundings but also for its genuine old beams.

The next group, on the main road, SHERWOOD, MERLINS, CANNONHURST, and BATLYNG MEDE are all on land which was bought by the builder, Smale, and are likely to have been built by him. They all date from 1935–38.

At this point we "look right, look left, look right again, and if it is safe we cross the road," (to quote the road-safety code taught to the young and their mums today.) Across Upper Bray Road, under the M4 flyover (a pang of regret to some of us that the Big Tree – an elm – at this corner had to be demolished) and on for 100 yards where we see BRAY COURT, another old house about to disappear. The story goes that this large Victorian house took four years to build and has 365 windows, one for each day of the year. Maybe . . . What is certain is that it was built by John Haig, of Scotch Whiskey fame.

"Haigs Folly" some called it because of its superluxurious materials and its vast entertaining rooms. In the drawing-room it was possible to carry on a conversation one end without any chance of being heard by those at the other end. The huge billiard room had a raised platform around the walls for guests to sit and chat without upset ting the concentration of the players. Only the finest mahogany was used for all interior woodwork, and all the appointments were of the same high standard.

There was no M4 in those days, so its grounds extended right through to the Upper Bray Road with stables, vinery, and gardener's cottage at that end. The Haigs also produced their own electricity, having a large and high water-tower for the purpose. Two Bray children went up to see it one day. The younger brother was enthralled by the huge tank and only escaped drowning, literally by the seat of his pants, when his elder sister pulled him back. She has 'had a thing' about water-tanks ever since!

The Haigs moved out after the first world war, when it was used for shell-shocked soldiers. In 1927 the estate was sold up, in lots, and thereafter the house saw a variety of occupants. In its time it has sheltered Spanish refugees (1936) Czechs (1939); been a girls' school, a boys' school; and latterly a store-house for a firm in Slough. In 1964 the last people to live in it moved out – a glimpse of its early glory remained in the form of two beautiful tapestries on the wall, which they were loth to leave there – (where are they now?). Thereafter the vandals and bats took over, though even in its derelict condition it has been useful. Several horror films have been made there, benefiting by ready-made thick cobwebs, broken boards and cracked windows.

Cookham RDC bought it five years ago, and have recently given permission for it to be pulled down. A housing development will fill the site of the house and what remains of its gardens.

Some open land, then BRAY RISE, a Victorian house built about 1885 and standing in an attractive garden with large trees. It is listed as "Farm" which probably dates from some 30 years ago, when it was bought by one of the Emmett family, for many years farmers in this area.

One more large house, BROOKMEAD, for which the owners have been kind enough to examine the deeds. We can, therefore, say "beyond a peradventure" that it was built by Mr. Timberlake in 1887, and sold at once to two sisters, the Misses Morrison. The story goes that they had a brother in the Army who would have used it for entertaining his friends, but he was killed in the Boer War. This might account for the design of the house – small bedrooms, and large ground-floor rooms and hall. A book of 1907 entitled "Contemporary Biographies" gives an account of the then owner, Mr. E.A. Radcliffe who was an architect at 9 High St., Maidenhead. Not only was he a remarkable all-round sportsman, and patented Radcliffe Skates but he was also an art-critic, and connoisseur and collector of antiques. A photograph shows "part of the valuable 'Hogarth' suite of Chippendale furniture" in his dining-room.

Thereafter the house had seven owners before the last sale in 1966.

It is of interest today to know that the owner of the land in 1887 sold it (1 acre of land) for £125.

The front garden has some beautiful trees standing in the lawn, and a driveway to the house which is well away from the road. The garden at the back with trees, shrubs, lawn and flower-beds is what house-agents describe as "mature" or "well-established."

Beyond it is a small shopping precinct, built in 1938 by Mrs. Mead. It contains a barber; bric-a-brac shop; grocer; and post office-cum-tobacconist-cum-newsagent. How long these and neighbouring houses will remain is doubtful. Many of the houses stand empty having been bought preparatory to a proposed large housing development surrounding the "lake" created by the gravel-diggers behind them. None are really large houses and some are quite small, but all have been 'home' during this century. There seems little point in recording them in detail.

Behind the shops stand the remains of an old tithe-barn. No accurate date is available as to its age, but it may well have been there for a couple of centuries.

A house which has certainly earned the right to be recorded is one now called BONDAI. It is 500 years old, having been the cottage for one of the woodmen of Windsor Forest. It probably had no name then but later it was

"Onions Farm." The original cottage of 3 small rooms is little changed, but there have been three new rooms added at the front, providing more light and space.

Its neighbour is younger and bigger. COMPTON CHASE has a curved drive sloping downhill from the road. Built about 1906 it is typical of its period and stands in 4 acres of garden. Its present owner has lived there for sixteen years and agrees with his neighbours at Bondai that they have no intention of moving! It is certainly to be hoped that some examples of earlier homes can be left *in situ*.

A previous owner of Compton Chase with less sense than sensibility gave a piece of his land to an old retainer to enable him to grow his own vegetables etc. Unfortunately he omitted to get it tied-up legally, so when a garage proprietor wanted to start business there it was quite simple for him, and the site has been used as such, under different owners, ever since. A new oblong building is being erected today.

A few more small houses with a doubtful life-span, a block of four council flats built in the past decade, and five houses built in the 1930's – and here we are at the boundary of the area – Clericus Hotel – Builders Cross – Monkey Island Lane.

PART THREE

PUBS & CLUBS

THE STAG AND HOUNDS

This is the only pub on the Braywick–Windsor Road section under review, and is lamentably short of records. Its present owner, Wethered's, have only two pieces of paper relating to it.

One dated 1814 states that it was "a dwelling house and carpenters shop owned by Mr. William Strugnell." The other, dated December 3rd 1845, is Wethered's purchase of the property from Mr. Hussey and Mr. Keene. One may presume that some time between the two dates it became a pub.

Towards the end of the last century a Mr. Vickery ran both the pub and the butcher's shop adjoining it. Two octogenarian memories who lived in the area as boys vouch for the slaughter-house behind it. Here both cattle and horses were killed. The youngsters would creep up quietly to watch the operations and stand there gaping in enjoyment until someone spotted them, threw some of the blood at them and shoo-ed them off. One of these blood-thirsty little horrors was also in demand for singing at the Working Men's Club meetings, held regularly in the pub, and on Sundays contributed to the "heavenly choir" in the church, bless 'im!

The present landlord of the pub, Mr. Balderson, has been there for seven years.

THE CROWN INN

It is thought that this dates from about 1380, which would make it the oldest building in Bray (except the Old Mill), even ante-dating the Lych gate. It was originally two cottages – the centre and right hand portions – but the other third of the building is not much younger.

Again, lamentably little appears to be recorded about the inn.

There is one tale current today that King Charles, when visiting Nell Gwynn, would ride to Braywick, then down the Causeway (which some still call King Charles' Causeway) and round to the Crown for a drink.

It has certainly been an inn for at least 200 years, as it is known that in George II's time a licence was granted to supply beer to the other cottages in the area. Drinks used to be served through the hatch in the wall, from a room behind it. The low ceilings and old beams must always have provided a snug atmosphere, as they do today. The left-hand cottage was incorporated, as a second bar, in 1956.

Crown Inn – 1972

Early this century there was a bicycle shop at the north end – bikes new and second-hand, and repairs. With the rough roads, there was probably a brisk trade in new tyres and puncture-patching.

The further end was a cottage in private occupation.

A full licence was granted in 1951, and the present landlord took over in 1959.

Recorded names and dates of landlords are:

Henry Sable	1893
Mr. South	1922
G. Parkin	1959

RINGERS INN

No positive statement can be made as to the date of this inn. It appears to have been always part of the line of cottages leading to the Lichgate, but as that was an inn, in the 18th century, it seems unlikely there would have been two in close proximity for a relatively small population. Maybe when "The Six Bells" ceased trading this cottage began providing the friendly pint.

About 1960–62 alterations revealed a considerable amount of wattle and daub, in common with the rest of the cottages, and the old beams contribute to the 15th–16th century picture. Some 17th and 18th century coins were uncovered at the same time.

Courages Brewery, Reading, were good enough to allow me to see such deeds as they possess. The following, if taken at a gallop, provides a good chase. I suggest a large sheet, or sheets, of paper, a thick pencil, and a pint at the elbow – to produce a record to be kept in The Ringers for all to see. A legal brain among the contributors might also help!

So, here is a run-down of the facts. There are gaps, but others may be able to fill them in.

The first deed is dated 1744, when the inn appears to pass rapidly from Thomas Christopher to John Martin to Elizabeth Christopher, who hands over in 1749 in an unreadable document possibly to Richard Tonson who surrenders "for ever" to John Hall in 1756. The same year the Bishop of Oxford gives up his rights, though how he ever came into the picture is nowhere stated! One more gasp in this century. In 1791 Richard Harsey goes before the ruling body, his "fealty" to the Lord of the Manor is "respited" and two good ladies Ann and Jane Buckland are installed. They must have sub-let to John Lawrence, John Burrows and Joseph Thomas Bell in the next 20 years, for in 1819 they surrender the copyhold premises to Abraham Ward, who obviously makes his will that year; Charles Pope is installed there in 1893 and 30 years later Mrs. Eleanor Lewis benefits. She, or her namesake, in 1896, is described as "of Castle Hill, Maidenhead" and leases to John Fuller, Brewer, "the Ringers, now used as a beerhouse" for 21 years at a rent of "£20 paid half-yearly in March and September."

She must have moved from Castle Hill to Bray, for she died at "The Cedars" (now Hanover House) in 1903 "possessed of a freehold house and a copyhold beerhouse with two cottages adjoining" (i.e. The Ringers and its adjoining cottages on the church side – now known as Oldfield View.)

James Woodhouse, gardener, and Henry Woodhouse of The Thames Hotel, Maidenhead, are her executors, and James Hayes is in occupation at the inn. They sell it to Thomas Story for £550. He becomes the lessee of the Fuller Story Company.

The following year, 1905, William H. Grenfell Esq., and others, grant the enfranchisement of the Ringers to him.

During most of these centuries the whole of the legal proceedings are conducted under the general "umbrella" of the Manor of Lowbrook.

It must have belonged to Nicholson and Sons in 1960, for it is they who arranged with Cookham R.D.C. for the installation of a lateral drain.

Courages took over in 1961–62.

The present hosts are Mr. and Mrs. George Ward.

THE HIND'S HEAD

Picture, if you will, two cottages facing south – probably first seeing the light of day in the 16th century – two rooms up, two down. At some unrecorded date the corner cottage became a small and cosy inn, remaining so until 1928. Deeds still in existence show some of the owners and lessees during the period 1801 to 1972.

1801 John Jennings sells to Thomas Auston, who raises a mortgage of £300 privately – presumably to buy it.
1807 Auston and George White sell to Basil Woodhouse, who sells in
1817 to John Lewis. He must have died by
1849 for his trustees sell to Benjamin Cliff.
1854 He sells to William Montagu Lamb Esq. who mortgages "house and land."
1865 Charles Pascoe Grenfell Esq., who was Lord of the Manor of Bray grants the enfranchisement to Mr. John Lewis. (The second of that name to hold it). Here there is a long gap in the records, for the next deed is
1928 when the whole scene changes. However, some of the gaps can be filled in from current memories and references. For instance
1893 Mrs. Woodhouse and her daughter ran it.
1910 Mrs. Plummer comes, from Monkey Island.
1914 Hewat is the inn-keeper.
1926 Hopkinson is there. Now we come to
1928 again, and the deed is between "Noakes & Co. Ltd., successor to Nevile Reid & Co. and Mr. Barry Neame. Tenancy at £52 p.a."

But we should look at the story leading up to this.

As a hotel and restaurant it all started with Kitty Henry. "Champagne Kitty" some called her. It was not a frivolous title, but more a tribute to her high standards in anything she undertook.

Hind's Head – 1929–30

Prior to coming to Bray she had inaugurated and managed two night-clubs in London which provided an ambience of quality and propriety, markedly at variance with the scores of less reputable places of entertainment in the capital during the 1920's. At the "Queen's Hall Roof" Jack Hylton was the pianist, then an unknown quantity to the public. His rise to fame began when Kitty Henry brought back from America a batch of jazz records which she asked him to orchestrate. This was a new "sound" in England, and rapidly caught on, as Kitty had foreseen.

A year or two later she started "Chez Henri", at Long Acre, where Charlie Kunz and Jack and Daphne Barker also rose to fame due to her encouragement, showing again her flair for recognising talent and quality. Bray was to benefit from her own talent within a few years.

Eventually tiring of the hurly burly of the London scene, she drove around the Thames Valley seeking some suitable place to open a restaurant.

In Bray she saw a small pub with a small cottage beside it. It was a cosy little place with a bar, and a table covered with a chenille cloth, an upright piano, and some chairs.

She liked it. She liked it very much. But it would have to be larger for her purpose.

The cottage adjoining, "Vine Cottage", belonged to Sir James Baird, then a bachelor, who used it only at week-ends when he was hunting with the Garth. He sold it to her, and she was then in business. By removing the centre wall, space was provided for serving meals within sight and sound of the bar.

In 1928 she engaged Barry Neame as hotel manager. Having been manager of the Savoy Laundry in London this was a new venture for him. However, the business prospered and before long a further expansion was needed. Beside the hotel was a passage-way leading to stabling at the back. This was filled, in record time, by the local builder, Mr. Sidney Gay, with a long dining-room.

Mr. Barry Neame introduced the idea of fine English food with extensive wine cellars, and in 1932 the cottage, No. 5 Church Street was bought for £350 and added to the hotel's back-stage working area. A 21 year lease of Bray Cottage, on the opposite side of the High Street, cost a further £400, plus rent of £150 p.a. Mr. Neame's enthusiasm seems to have outrun his judgement about now for he borrows £1,000 at 5% from John Gardner (London) Ltd. But he had created a meeting place for royalty and film stars, and The Hind's Head was "on the map" nationally and internationally. Sir Alfred Munnings became his close friend, and painted a portrait of him dining in the garden with "an un-named lady." Though not one of Sir Alfred's chefs d'oeuvres it is of interest today, and hangs in the hotel. The two men thoroughly enjoyed the gay scene and the food and wine, but profits disappeared down willing gullets and eventually the creditors closed in.

One of these was John Gardner Ltd., who took over in 1940.

They retained Barry Neame for a further year and then appointed his secretary, Miss Lois Williams in his place.

This proved to be a very good move, for she ran the hotel

entirely successfully for nearly 30 years, becoming a much-loved and internationally famous lady. Royalty and film stars continued to come; Etonians and their parents were regular visitors; The Hunt met outside on Boxing Days for their stirrup cups; and business-men impressed clients by dining and wining them in such famous and enjoyable surroundings.

The culmination of her career was to have Her Majesty Queen Elizabeth and H.R.H. Prince Philip entertain some five Queens and foreign dignitaries to lunch on the eve of Princess Alexandra's wedding. The speciality of that day was saddle of lamb and the well-known treacle tart. The guest list and photographs of the Royal party arriving by coach are framed and hang in the lounge. So, too, is the original of a Giles Cartoon sparked-off by the amusing incident of the hurried removal of a sign outside stating "No Coaches Allowed"!

The acquisition of Bray Cottage and its large garden in 1931 was from Richard Lewis Esq. Photographs exist of the property in 1867 when it was owned by John Lewis and was only of two storeys. It is not known today when the top floor and mansard roof were added, except that it was certainly more than 50 years ago. In 1867 the windows facing the High St., had been bricked in. There was a portico with pillars at the front door, facing north, and a room built out over it. The range of buildings behind were only single-storey and used for storage; the roof was pitched and tiled (a small portion remains today, visible from the yard of Bray Garage).

The deed of conveyance of 1931 contains a plan of all the buildings, calling the property "The Garden House," which is somewhat confusing today as "The Garden House Flat" refers to a building further up the drive, facing south, which was once the coach-house and groom's quarters. Mr. Charles Gardner lived in it during the last war, and subsequent managers have done like-wise.

The large garden was always beautifully kept, meals

1870 Cottages, Hibbert Road, 1972

Hind's Head – Early Thirties

Ferry and Charlese – circa 1883

The Ferry – Thirties

Ferry Road – 1905

George Hotel, Bray – 1907

Thames Villa. Bray residence of Tot Saunders Head sweeping Trade merchant. Bray church in corner of picture.

In the "Stables" behind the Villa E.T.W. & W.C.W. were born (approximate date) | E.T. Williams March 3rd 1899. W.C. Williams May 5th 1902. Boer War ended 28 days after I was born!

"Braydene" built to replace Thames Villa about 1905–6. Italian craftsmen put in the floors. The interior was lavishly decorated but was never so happy as in the old Villa. We left the Stables in 1909–10 … [illegible]
… [illegible]

Ferry Road, 1972

View from Top of Parish Church looking south – circa 1900

High Street, Bray – 1900

Bray Court – 1973

Bray Bank – 1972

being served on the lawn when weather permitted. There are still some fine old trees, including a mulberry producing an abundant crop of fruit.

In 1968 Mrs. Marla Kelly took over the house for the Gardner family after the retirement of Miss Williams and a substantial amount of improvement work has been carried out since in an attempt to regain the atmosphere and service of its former days. The public bar has been altered giving a more spacious lounge and new bar for added customer comfort.

A new staircase in Columbian pine was designed by Mr. Alan Hills and constructed to give easy access to the upstairs Royal Room, together with a new Reception area with a central wine cellar immediately behind.

The old 'Fourposter' bedroom and bathroom have been transferred across the road to the Garden House and the old plaster ceiling has been removed, exposing the original rafters and beams, to form the new "Vicar's Room" for private dinner parties.

The ground floor of The Garden House was opened as a Coffee House in 1971.

THE ALBION

In Old Mill Lane (formerly called Monkey Island Lane) this inn was built about 1850 by Mr. Mickley to house the bargees who brought coal and timber to the wharf. At that time there was a channel running from the river inland through land beside the site of Charmian and Wytch House but not reaching the Lane. The goods were stacked between the wharf and the inn and provided a popular playground for the children clambering over them. Not so popular with their overworked mothers when they arrived home with coal-smutched clothes, though!

Mr. Mickley obtained a beer licence so that the bargees could have a good meal, a drink and sleep before their return journeys.

One unique, if small, feature is that it is the only building in Bray with an inscribed Ordnance Survey mark.

Mr. Mickley was also the village carpenter, builder and undertaker in the early 1900's, and other members of his family were active in the village for many years before him. They owned all the land from the Ferry to the Mill property (today's River Gardens boundary.)

WATERSIDE INN

The history here is somewhat complicated to follow, but we'll try.

The original Waterside was on the opposite side of Ferry Road, where Linum Cottage now stands.

This inn was then called "The George Inn." The house probably dated from the 18th century, when it was a private house called "Charlese." By 1893 it was an inn.

Early in this century it became increasingly popular with the more rowdy elements of "the gentry and officers" who came from London for week-ends or just for the night.

One incident caused much amusement in the village. At the end of a riotous evening the staff discovered what appeared to be an old man collapsed under the table, but when they picked 'him' up they found it was a lady minus her wig!

The inn became notorious for its wine, women, and song, and was eventually raided by the police and its licence removed.

It was then sold for use again as a private house, reverting to "Charlese."

In 1948 the brewery who owned the "Waterside" bought it, and were given permission to transfer their licence and name to the present inn. (They sold the original small Waterside as a private house.)

It has changed hands many times since then, but never

again lost its licence!

The present owners have added a glass-walled restaurant in which one can enjoy the river-scene, uninterrupted by other buildings, whatever the temperature outside. Set into the wall beneath it are old iron rings which must have provided mooring for some half-dozen punts in days gone by.

CLUBS (VARIOUS)

From the '20s to the '40s there were several 'clubs' in the centre of the village.

Membership was a nominal 5s, an "entry fee" which gave one the opportunity to spend far larger sums on drinks and gambling, for which there was also a charge for "table-money."

Ferry End had several such clubs, including No. 1 and No. 3 and the Isis Club at what is now Needham Lodge, and in Bettoney Vere No. 6 which was mostly for Bridge evenings.

At "Two Ways Cottage" there was a tennis club, as well as drinks and cards.

Those in the village today who knew it then will tell that "there must have been a score or more. Can't remember all of them now, but there was a brisk trade in providing for them."

Altogether Bray had quite a "reputation" at that time, as indeed, had Marlow and Maidenhead.

MAIDENHEAD AND BRAY SPORTS CLUB

This title dates only from 1945 when it "was born, a weak and somewhat sickly child, from some private correspondence between two friends not then demobilised."

Its roots, however, are in the Maidenhead Cricket Club of 1798 when they played at Oldfield (a field on the east side of the junction of Forlease Road and Oldfield Road). Many matches were played, including contests with the MCC – Kerry records that "on one of these occasions, the Londoners retired in high dudgeon on hearing the (church) bells sound their defeat, and refused to partake of an excellent collation provided for them at Bray."

Not only did activities cease in the first world war, but the terrible casualties of that holocaust had their effect on the re-building of a strong club. In 1920 the Advertiser reported of a match "The Club is but a shadow of its former self," and it was not until 1926 that it had fully recovered.

The inter-war years were fraught with difficulties over playing-grounds and finance, which were showing signs of abating in 1939 when the Club "had once more to put up its shutters."

The idea of a joint Sports Club had been mooted in 1879, but not until 1938 was any concrete plan put forward. With the interruption of the '39–'45 war this had to be shelved.

The summer of 1946 saw the Maidenhead and Bray Cricket Clubs playing as one Club. By the winter of that year the Maidenhead Hockey Club joined the group and in 1948 they could boast a membership of some 250 playing and non-playing members. In that year there were five men's hockey teams, two ladies' hockey teams and two cricket elevens. They were finding that the ground at Bray "cannot stand the strain of the two sports, winter and summer." This is the year of the 150th anniversary of the Cricket Club. During the cricket week, August 1st–7th matches were played against Byfleet, Eton Masters, Berkshire Gentlemen, Maidenhead and District local clubs, Hampshire Club and the MCC led by Mr. (*sic*) C.E. Mott-Radcliffe M.P. The Friday match was followed by the Anniversary Ball on the lawn of Bray Vicarage, by kind permission of the Rev. E.S.C. Lowman.

The club first came to Bray village in 1919, taking over the large field previously known as Gaskins (or Garston's) Mead which had been in constant use for pasturing cattle.

There had been two watering-places for the animals, one near Sawkins Bridge (leading to the Fisheries) and the other between "Riverside" and "Little Basing." The latter remained open until 1962 when Mr. Pickering fenced it in with his garden.

From 1919 to 1962 the Club had rented the ground from the Church, but they wanted it as a permanency and set about raising the money for its purchase. This they accomplished by prodigious efforts. The owner of Riverside, on Vicarage Walk, bought the strip of land from his house to the main road, which is also used by the Club, as access to his building.

The old pavilion, part of which still stands, was replaced by a large new building which was completed, and opened, in 1968. It comprises the River Room (used for dining, dancing etc) and bar; a large kitchen; two changing-rooms; and two showers. As well as being used for the Club's activities it can be hired for outside functions.

The membership is now approximately 400, males and females, with 14 hockey teams and three cricket elevens, and there is training for young people in both sports.

The large tree near the road was included in a map of 1875, and is still a glorious sight in a crisp autumn.

BRAY VILLAGE HALL AND CLUB

Originally called "Bray Memorial Hall" it was designed by Mr. West Neve and was to be a memorial to those who died in the 1914–18 war.

Bray needed a hall for its increased population. The Old Schoolroom had been used for some social activities but this hall provided more space and more facilities as a social centre.

The funds for its building were raised by private subscription and a considerable part of the outstanding sum was provided by a "grand opening night" in 1922 when

Dame Nellie Melba gave her services free. Memories relate that "she wore a blue taffeta dress, with a large pink rose at the waist, and was brought by Mr. Schuster in his Rolls Royce." The hall was packed, tickets selling at a guinea a time.

The interior was furnished and equipped by Sir Hugo and Lady Cunliffe-Owen, of Weirbank. From the beginning there has always been a management committee – the Rev. Riddelsdell and Captain Beattie being two of the original committee of eight. There were weekly whist drives and dances, with the bar in the small room at the entrance until 1924. In that year the Social Club was added. A billiard-table, darts and bar provided amusement and companionship, and led to participation in snooker tournaments. Mr. Balsam, of Maidenhead, presented the first silver cup in 1924 which was won by W.C. Howes; the latest winner was Mr. R. Green, The Terrace. Several other trophies adorn the shelves behind the bar.

The summer of 1928 saw another party. This was on the occasion when Sir Hugo Cunliffe-Owen's "Felstead" won the Derby. As he had been bred at Weir Bank Stud Farm the whole village rejoiced. Flags and bunting decked the houses and roads, rivals forgot their aggressions, and all joined in the celebrations. Inside the Hall champagne flowed; Dame Nellie Melba sang again; those not in the Hall sang in the pubs, and many a head troubled its owner next morning!

In 1928 the Women's Institute held its first meeting in the Hall, with Lady Benson of Chauntry House as President, where it has continued ever since. That is to say, with the exception of the years 1939–45 when it was closed to social activities, and used for packing aircraft spare parts.

In 1946 it was re-opened for the village. The Maidenhead and Bray Boxing Club used it twice a week from 1956–66 for training sessions and latterly for running two tournaments each year.

Mr. Jack Jeans was on the committee in 1946, and became Secretary of the Club in 1956. For more than 20 years he and Mrs. Knibbs have served the bar for three nights each per week, Mrs. Knibbs doing the cleaning as well. Their services have been much appreciated.

Membership over the years has waxed and waned, averaging about 50. It is now down to 30 members, as most of the younger generation prefer the atmosphere of discotheques and modern dancing. The bar turnover and billiards have formed the only financial support.

With the licence due to expire in 1974 urgent action was called for. It was therefore decided to hand it over to the Village Hall Committee who managed to raise the requisite membership to allow of the club's continuation. Its bar is still an asset for any dances in the Hall, and its other activities may well be welcomed in an age of increasing leisure.

In 1968 the Management Trustees resigned. An elected committee arranged the conditions whereby the Hall could be registered with the Charity Commissioners. This involved electing a committee consisting of one representative from each of the organisations in the village (e.g. Church Council, W.I. etc.) with an equal number of non-representative inhabitants, elected at each Annual General Meeting.

This body of people set about raising funds for a complete re-furnishing of the interior. Many events were organised and, with added financial help from the Bray Parish Council, it was possible by 1972 to,

(a) equip the stage with all necessities for productions;
(b) lay a new floor;
(c) modernise the kitchen;
(d) remake the toilets;
(e) re-decorate the interior; and
(f) install oil-fired central heating.

The exterior is now being repaired and re-decorated, and a new entrance porch (designed by Mr. Alan Hills) constructed to replace the rapidly disintegrating original one.

All these efforts have brought about a fuller community spirit in the village. The first officers on this committee were: Chairman – Mr. Ken Dudley; Secretary – Mr. Charles Birney; Treasurer – Mr. C. Dew.

The hall is used regularly by the Women's Institute; the Multiple Sclerosis Society, who have a monthly tea-party for disabled people drawn from a broad area; a pre-school play-group which caters for the under-fives on four mornings a week. It is also booked for private parties, weddings etc.

HOTEL DE PARIS

Though this was neither club nor pub it should hold some place in the records of the 20th century since it was famous in its day, and provided "jest and youthful jollity" to wealthy visitors, and employment to some of the villagers.

The house called Braymead was built in 1901–2 by Mr. F.I. Pitman, a stockbroker, and official starter for the Oxford and Cambridge boat race. He lived here in the grand manner, with carriages, footmen, and all the rest of a staff necessary for such a domain. When he left, about 1922, several local people formed a syndicate to run it as a hotel. The great auction sale of properties in 1923 took place at what was then Braymead Hotel, but the venture never really went well.

In 1928 it started its famous career as the "Hotel de Paris" deriving the name from its new owners Mr. Poulson and Mr. Stocco who were running the Café de Paris in London.

On the river-side there was a large glass terrace-restaurant taking 14 tables. It was used most often in the summer when it could get very hot, so a constant cascade of water was poured over the glass roof to cool it.

Dancing could be either in an indoor ballroom taking 150 people, or on an open-air dance floor on the lawn for 100.

The American bar was created from Mr. Pitman's gun-room, and the 10 garages beside the Albion from the stables.

Top-ranking bands and cabaret stars from the Café de Paris entertained the 2–300 visitors at week-ends, who included many famous names both British and foreign, film and stage.

It was the age of the Bright Young Things who lived it up as riotously as the Naughty Nineties had done. On one of the rowdiest occasions when glass, china, and flower-pots had been hurled around, the manager became very anxious about a large glass showcase containing antique silver and jewellery. All the porters and waiters were called in to form a protective ring around it, but this was too much for the head-waiter, who had a heart attack and had to be removed to the office, poor man!

A regular booking was the Guards' passing-out-parade party from Camberley when there would be 4–500 guests. At midnight there was always a lemming-like jump into the river by the males, clothed or unclothed but very discreetly behind the shrubbery!

Neither here nor at the Hinds Head were coach-parties welcomed, but an exception was made for a golden-wedding party. The host explained that he wanted his guests to be able to drink as much as they liked and to be transported home, each to his own house – a very considerate gesture which appealed to the hotel manager, so the party plans went ahead.

Other tales of that period are best left untold – but there was at least one permanent effect in the village. The name of the house on the corner of Brayfield Road was changed from "Corner Cottage," to "Careless Corner," due to guests leaving their parties and being unable to decide "the way to go home."

Black-out, petrol rationing and belt-tightening in 1939 put an end to the night-life, and it was taken over by a shipping insurance company from London for the duration.

With the return of peace came the return of hotel activities but never again on the same scale as before. Gradually its name and fame dwindled until at last it was sold, pulled down, and replaced by the flats and houses of Braybank in 1964.

PART FOUR

WATER, WATER, EVERYWHERE

A history of Bray's houses would not, at first sight, require any report on the river. Yet the river was here before any houses and has played its part in developments throughout the years. (There is one theory tenaciously held by its advocates, that Bray was once an island.)

Bray reach, when mentioned at all, has been accorded a mere wave of the hand while in transit between Maidenhead and Windsor. When I asked the Queen's Swan-Master, Captain John Turk, for an account of it his immediate reply was "There isn't much to say. Bray is a part one passes *through.*" (In much the same vein, Berkshire historians imply that Bray was an area one passed *by*!)

That may have been the case in earliest times too, for there are no known remains of habitation nearer to the village than Down Place, and man may well have passed by the "bogges" to get to the ford linking Berks with Bucks, where later there was to be a ferry. As late as 1843 the report of this reach is that "the shallows are very frequent and the current very strong" so this would have been one of the shallows.

Fishing has always gone on, providing food for the fishermen, and levies and tithes, to the Sovereigns and the local clergy. Fish weirs are said to have existed at several places along the reach; at Garstons Meadow, Bray Vicarage, Headpile Ait, Bray Mill and Monkey Island. The last of the fishing-bucks are said to have disappeared by 1890, though an account of 1901 refers to "eel-bucks with a boat near by on the bank."

This could have been one marked on a map of 1875 as "Fishweir and Waterfall" just below Sawkins Bridge, for an island was then in the making in mid-stream at that point – not a large one, but big enough by 1918 for people to fish from it.

One boy used to do just that, with friends. It is deeply engraved on his memory as this story will show.

Returning from school in Maidenhead he had chatted and played with friends, and realised he was going to be late getting home. With his conscience ill at ease within, and dark clouds overhead he hurried through the Fisheries. At Sawkins Bridge there was a terrific clap of thunder which scared him still more. To crown it all, as he crossed he saw a huge swell of water sweep over, engulf, and wash away "his" fishing island. This was the last straw, and he legged-it for home, white and terrified. "Conscience" may "make cowards of us all" but he had had more than enough for one day!

A curious feature of this island, vouched for by others and marginally visible in two paintings, is that the Thames Conservancy has no record of it, or of its remains being dredged, in this century.

The only other visible sign of old-time fishing is at Monkey Island. There, when the river is low one can see the remains of a built-up carp-pool, off the up-river part of the island.

Today's fishing is a pastime enjoyed by anglers on the Bucks bank, and the occasional youngster in somebody's garden on this side, as Bray has no public access to the river today, except at the "ferry" where there is still the right to water cattle.

The old mill was another user of the river from Domesday or earlier. Thacker says that in 1770 it was called "Levell's paper-mill," and in 1794 "Lavender's, for corn." Certainly during the 19th century and the first decade of the 20th the river was the power for "grinding flour of an excellent quality."

As a means of transporting goods and people it has been in constant use. Probably hides from "the Furest" were sent to Bray's tannery (see Old Tan House); wood, flour, and flax could have been "exports"; much later in the 18th and 19th centuries, the wharf dealt with coal and building materials; and the weir at the mill was in constant use for barges plying further afield. Several of the millers had complaints lodged against them "for taking excessive toll"! Once the lock was built, in 1845, river traffic no longer used the mill's water, though the lock was only used at low water at first, and no tolls were taken at high water when the lock was left open at both ends. The Conservancy took control in 1866, and while there is still the tow-path on the Bucks-bank, no craft is horse-drawn and the path is for pedestrians only. It has suffered erosion of some 10 feet in the past two centuries.

Of recent years there has been an annual competition for the best-kept lock. Bray's Mr. Baldwin had such a beautiful floral display that he won it nine times between 1959 and 1969. The present lock was built in 1885 in a slightly different position from the old one.

Barge traffic suffered a decline with the extension of railway transport in the 19th century. Nevertheless there was still business to be done, and Bray's wharf dealt regularly with coal and wood which was stacked beside the Albion Inn (q.v.). Mr. C. Mickley owned all the land from the Ferry to the present River Gardens, all of it being open for grazing except the wharf area.

The main use of the river from the last half of the 19th century has been increasingly for recreation and sport. Such barges as there are, work for the dredging of the channel and have to take the gravel and soil far afield rather than dumping it on the bank, which was their previous practice.

Rowing, paddling and punting became de rigueur; and houseboats appeared, moored to the banks. Two such were at Bray. "The Shamrock," near Sawkins Bridge, became a well-known 'club' for some years before the 14–18 war; while "The Sunbeam," moored at the up-river boundary of the Vicarage garden provided slightly less exciting leisure occupations.

Rowing as a competitive sport was linked in the earlier years with Marlow, but with the formation of Maidenhead Rowing Club in 1876 the Bray reach was in constant use for training and eventually for the Maidenhead Regatta which takes place today at the end of July. The course for the races is between Sawkins Bridge and Maidenhead Railway Bridge, but the crews paddle down as far as the Vicarage before turning towards the starting point. Here it is that they "stiffen the sinews; summon up the blood" for the contest ahead. Local residents volunteer to chug around in their motor-launches like determined sheep-dogs when mustering competitors, or as guard-dogs when warning-off through traffic. Bray, too had its regattas this century, but only for punting. They were gay occasions with punts moored full-across the river, so that one could walk from Berks to Bucks dry-shod.

The Woodhouse family contributed to punting-fame, one being a national lady-champion and another designing and making first-class punts for both leisure and for racing. At Regatta-time there was jollification on Bray Green in the evenings as well as the parties in private houses. Today it is rare to see a punt in these waters and rarer still to see one being poled. The boatyard stopped its punts-to-hire and electric canoes in 1959. The wash from faster, motorised craft used to swamp them, which certainly reduced the enthusiasm of their passengers, let alone the obliterating of any would-be romantic ideas!

Today's languid ladies prefer to drape themselves well above water on the decks of cruisers; draperies have given way to bikinis; and the peace of the punt has given way to the pace of the put-put.

Geoffrey Messum's boat-yard concentrated entirely on a fleet of motor-cruisers for hire by day, week, or month. They also berthed and repaired privately-owned boats.

The origins of the ferry, the boat-yard, the boat-house,

call it what you will lie, as we have seen, in the wharf, and in two generations of Mickleys. It was the first who built the house called THE RYEPECK (a ryepeck is "an ironshod pole for securing punts" C.O.D.). It appears on a map of 1875.

The large house on the river at the bottom of Ferry Road, called FERRY COTTAGE was built after 1883 by Charles Mickley the younger as a private house, and leased to various tenants until about 1910 when it was taken over by C.E. Hughes for use as a business concerned with boat building and boat-hiring.

He was certainly one of Bray's "characters" in his time. Everyone remembers him as "Whacker Hughes" – the nickname being connected with his prowess in his business and his punting. He was also a good shot and a formidable drinker. The tale is told, with amusement, that he could be more than half-seas-over and still get a left-and-a-right at a brace of pigeon – provided he was held upright and a loaded gun put in his hands!

He retained the business until 1923 when a family well-known for centuries on the Thames moved to Bray from Richmond. R.H. Messum bought the business and properties but did not live there for three years (when Whacker died). He and his family were at Needham Lodge, Ferry Road.

The boatyard was mainly concerned with hiring, his son Geoffrey taking over and continuing it from 1946 until his untimely death in 1971. His passing was keenly felt by all who knew him both on the river and in the village.

The boats and equipment were sold in 1972 and the landing stages dismantled. The house will be auctioned in April this year (1973).

FLOODS

Though sweet Thames usually runs softly there have been

times when it has run riot.

The earliest recorded flooding was in 1877 but 1894 still holds the record for height and extent of water.

In Bray almost all of the houses were flooded, their inhabitants having to live in the upstairs rooms. Essential foods and milk were delivered by boat, and Mr. Marks delivered letters by attaching them to the end of his horsewhip to hand up to people at their windows. Supplies of goods had to be by boat from Maidenhead, whether in large strong punts or in rowboats.

The village has always been threatened by water from two directions, the river coming inland, and the higher land draining downwards. This has meant flooding to a greater or lesser extent in many winters. School-children became accustomed to going to Braywick school by punt from the Causeway to the bottom of the hill in Hibbert Road. In those days the road was much lower, with a deep dip beside Gaskins Mead (Sports Club). Here the water was frequently up to the horses' bellies, and a notice would be put up on the village side warning that the depth of water was too great for ponies. Any would-be riders would then use the telegraph pole on the corner of the Green as a hitching-post, and continue their journey by punt. On Sunday afternoons an enterprising boatman provided trips by punt to Maidenhead and back.

A warning of imminent flooding was the arrival in the High Street of the swans. Formerly considered prescience it is now known that this is because the current in the river is running too strongly, and their home on Headpile Eyot being swamped, so they seek shelter on higher ground, and stomp their way up Ferry Road to the village.

The year after the Great Flood was memorable as being the year of the Great Freeze. The Bray reach was frozen almost bank to bank with just a small channel in the centre where the river moved. Parties were held on the ice, with hot sausages, chestnuts and oranges on sale; it was estimated that the thickness of the ice would take the weight of

Eel bucks

a horse and trap and Mr. Marks was invited to test the assertion – an invitation he refused politely but firmly. Ice-hockey was played on the backwater behind the Headpile Eyot, and the mill-wheel ceased its gyrations.

In 1947 the floods were almost as bad, the water reaching the top of the steps at 'Red Eyot', Hibbert Road, and the fields each side of the Causeway were a good three feet deep in water. Heavy snow for weeks before-hand thawed in March and emptied into the river. It was possible to punt all the way from Bray to Cookham, passing on the way houses with their front doors open and craft tied up at the bottom of the stairs. Shoppers in Bridge Street, Maidenhead, had to use cat-walks constructed of planks supported on brick columns.

Thereafter flood levels have been recorded in 1954, 1959, and 1960 but never so extensive as the earlier ones.

The re-routing and deepening of the Cut has made a

great improvement in Bray's conditions in wet weather; drawing off much of the flooding from Braywick and Canon Hill before it reaches the lower fields and the village. It is unlikely that another fish will be caught outside Mr. Jones' shop as it was in 1894!

We should not leave this part of the river without mentioning the oldest of all the "families" – the swans. Generations of them have nested regularly on Headpile Eyot. As is fitting for Bray 'which belonged to the Sovereign' the single pair have always been royal property. Their territory extends to a position level with "The Old Coach House" and is fiercely and vociferously guarded from intruders. No matter how great the housing-shortage the cob appears each Spring, armed cap-à-pie in mighty wrath, to do battle and to win.

Every year, in July, they are recorded during swan-upping. For 500 years the Sovereign's swan-master, accompanied by representatives of the Vintners and Dyers Companies, has sailed the full length of the river checking and recording the swans and their cygnets.

Bray has one pair on Headpile Eyot, and another at Monkey Island.

Now, through the lock, with its island, early called Parting Eyot and later Parton Ait; past the millrace; past Monkey Island with its old carp-pool, and backwater bridged in 1956; on to Queen's Eyot.

Why Queen's? Probably because many of the Kings owning Bray, gave it to their spouses – hence Queen's Eyot here and "The Queen's Head" public house not far away, on the Windsor Road.

Since 1898 it has belonged to Eton College. They made up the banks and planted trees on it, and in 1900 built and opened the pavilion. It is used by the Etonians during the summer only, for rest and refreshment either at the end of a water-journey or as half-way house on a longer stint. Scullers, eights and fours, Oxford gigs, whiffs and dodgers all find their way here.

It is not as quiet and leisurely a pursuit today, as the river-traffic is increasing so rapidly. Small, medium and large motorised craft predominate, the largest being the steamers plying between Windsor and Mapledurham, their top decks crowded with trippers, and pop-music competing with the noise of the engine. It is tempting to wander on, but this is the end of our area, and we must return to the hinterland.

PART FIVE

LOCAL GOVERNMENT

The clerk of the Cookham Rural District Council, Mr. J.R. Eley, F.I.A.C. has kindly provided the following notes showing the birth and growth of local government.

"The history of the parish as a unit of local administration goes back well into the manorial system. In later years the meetings were held under the auspices of the local parson and became known as the vestries. In 1601 the vestries received their first legal power – that of levying a poor rate for the district and administering poor relief. However, by the middle of the 19th century their powers had declined considerably and by the Local Government Act 1894 Parish Councils, as they are known today, were established. This Act transferred the remaining civil functions of the older Parish authorities to the new institutions. Their constitution and membership are now governed by the Local Government Act 1933. The Cookham R.D.C. held its first Council Meeting on January 2nd, 1895."

The extracts from the Minutes of Bray Parish Council's A.G.M's give some indication of matters for concern in this area. Attendance at these meetings was never very good, proportionate to the increase in population remaining about the same until the late 1960's, when, thanks to the Skeffington Report at Westminster advocating more local participation and co-operation, and also the regular attendance of our local councillors at the Bray Preservation Society's meetings the local citizenry began to take heart and realise that "the faceless ones" were not as unapproachable as the pessimists asserted and that the local wishes would be listened to and, where possible, their needs supplied. Today the village is regaining much of its pre-

1920 entity and unity; more of the young-marrieds are taking their share of responsibility for their present and future; and there is a growing awareness of the importance of this with the imminent re-organisation of the whole country into large local government areas. Parish Councils and amenity societies will have to be the watch-dogs, bark and bite, for local communities.

Extracts from Bray Parish Council Minutes

1894. The welfare and management of local affairs passes from the hands of the clergy and a few "overseers" drawn from the landed gentry into a properly constituted Council to be elected by ratepayers. On October 31st the last meeting is held under the old aegis when it is "Resolved that the Vicar and Henry Adams Esq call upon Mr Alfred Fossick, Solicitor, and ask him to give a lecture in explanation of the Local Government Act, 1894."

The first meeting took place in the Old Schoolroom, Bray on December 4th 1894 when Chas. Wm. Cox was elected as first Chairman, with 12 Councillors.

They dealt with the whole Parish, as now, but I have extracted from the minutes of the Annual General Meetings items mostly concerning Bray Town and Braywick.

At the 1895 meeting "There was a large number of ratepayers, including two ladies – the Misses Raymond, sister and daughter of the Vicar." One wonders why. Were they a radical family, daring to appear in what had always been a male preserve, or was it simply that the Vicar felt the need of their support on that particular day? It was unusual enough to warrant a comment in the Minutes, anyway.

Their regular business included the administering of various Charities and Gifts, two of which dealt with specified areas. Wm. Levetts (Lichgate) Charity – and the Cherry Charity which were, and are, connected with the lichgate, and schools and educational grants.

In 1896 other charities provided, inter alia:

248 lbs. Meat £7.14s
90 loaves bread £1.10s
Number of recipients 172
288 cwt. of coals at 19s per ton

Delivered to 288 cottages.

Clothing and shoes to girls of Touchen End School and Braywick School.

Flannel for poor £5.16s

At this meeting also began a long discussion about the location of a Burial Ground, which was not finally resolved and executed until 1906 when the last of the bills was paid for the present cemetery in Windsor Road.

In 1900 Cookham R.D.C. is taken to task for the unsatisfactory condition of the footpath from Jesus Hospital to the crossroads at Bray Court. "Mr. Eggleton said he had spoken to the road foreman about the need for new trunks etc . . . but without any good result."

Tempers must have run high for a year. At the next meeting, 1901 they resolve that they "are of the opinion that the Rural District of Cookham for parochial purposes is a complete failure" and that they will petition their M.P. (of Wokingham) to have the road-conditioning "removed from the R.D.C. and returned to the Parish Council's care, which had always previously been highly satisfactory."

They also voted £15 for "Lighting and Watching" under the Act of 1833, and it is interesting to note that the village is till being referred to as Bray Town.

There must have been gates each end of the Causeway, for in 1907 the ratepayers ask why they have been replaced by barriers. Answer: "to keep cattle off the pathway and to allow perambulators to be taken along." This does not go down well and they resolve to request the R.D.C. to give them back the gates. Two years later they complain of bicycles being ridden there, being a danger to pedestrians. (There is no record of successful measures to control the nuisance, and today we still rack our brains for a solution).

The lamps in the village during the winter months of 1911 were much appreciated, and a request was made "that this be continued for a little longer."

Reference is made to "the new road called Brayfield Road," coupled with a request for drainage between this and Poulton's shop, "the shop at the Terrace." The request was granted that year. By 1912 the lane was drained.

Immediately, another request. A fresh coating of tar for "the road." This pre-supposes a previous tarring, which is not recorded. In 1913 some people have asked for permission "to enclose Holmans Mat, the plot of greensward in front of The Old Dutch House, with posts and chains." This was opposed vehemently and unanimously. Motion lost. Again there are complaints of cycles (motor-cycles this time), on the Causeway and demands for posts each end to baulk them.

Comes the first world war. In 1915 Mr. Jones, dealing with Penystone Charity said that "£25 had been allotted for apprenticing a lad, but owing to the European War it was difficult to find him a master as so many were away in the King's service."

In 1916 and 1917 meetings had to be in the cottage-end of the Old Schoolroom "in consequence of the Order as to Lights", and very few attended. With the peace came a return to the Old Schoolroom; the resignation of Mr. A. Marks and Mr. T.J. Digby, both of whom had served on the council for some years; and unfavourable comments on the drainage of roads and ditches throughout the Parish.

On, then, to the '30s when Canon Jones, the well-loved Vicar, takes part in the proceedings.

Mention is made of the need to repair "the seat under the Big Tree". The capital letters are valid since this was a recognised land-mark for generations. On the first Ordnance Survey map of 1871 it is marked as Big Elm. It grew at the corner of Holyport Road and Windsor Road and was one of the casualties of modern "progress." That is, the

M.4 necessitated its slaughter, and its "passing" was felt as a personal loss to many of us.

In 1934 Mr. Cox resigned after 40 years on the council, from its first meeting. A long and valuable service to the community.

Electric light in the school figures in the minutes of 1941, and in 1946 there is a request for "the extension" (*sic*) of electric lighting in the street of Oakley Green and Fifield. So we may assume that Bray already had it.

1960–62. Main drainage was installed in Bray. A temporary, if real, inconvenience and expense to those receiving it (it was not compulsory immediately) but a welcome improvement on the old cess-pool emptying. From 1962–65 arguments and plans for Bray Close (previously the site of "The Little House") and worries over heavy lorries through the village bring a better attendance at meetings. In 1966 a new footpath is made beside Bray Green.

The meeting of 1968 really brought in the ratepayers. Oakley Green Allotments had been sold to the Ministry of Defence for £23,000 and the Parish was "in the money" for the first time ever! What should be done with it? Many and varied were the claims and suggestions both as to its investment and as to its immediate spending. Only one decision could be taken there and then – fair shares for each village was essential.

Bray's first slice of the cake took the form of improving Bray Green, which was completed by 1970. There was also a grant to the Village Hall towards the cost of internal improvements.

In 1972 a "Village Plan" was discussed. This had been produced by the Bray Preservation Society in conjunction with a professional area-planner subsidised by the Council. It is now lodged with the County Council, at their request, to assist them in (we hope) preserving Bray as a village.

From 1894 to today the charities are administered. Educational grants still go out from the Cherry Charity; the Lichgate is maintained; and the Bray Parish Charities supply coal and groceries. The original meat and bread allocations ceased in that form in 1940.

Conservation Area

The Government Amenities Act of 1967 produced in Bray, via the Berks County Council and Cookham R.D.C., a conservation area entitled "Bray Village to Braybank. Area No. 4." This was registered in 1968. Its boundaries include most of Maidenhead and Bray Sports Club; crossing at Hog Bridge; curving South East taking in Jesus Hospital; then West including Hanover Mead; curving North East to the bounds of, but excluding, Braybank; thence back along the river to the Sports Club area, though it does not include Little Basing and Riverside or Vicarage Walk. The curved and thick lines make it difficult to pin-point sections of open fields.

LISTED BUILDINGS

	Grade	*Date*
Rickhams	II	18th century
The Old Dutch House	II	15th century
Monkey Island	I	15th century
Vicarage Cottage	II	15th century
St. Michael's Church	A	12th century
Chauntry Chapel	II	15th century
Jesus Hospital	I	1627
Chauntry House	II	mid 18th century and later
Charmian and Wytch House (formerly known as Two Ways)	II	1920
Stuart Cottage	II	15th or 16th century
Shottery (formerly Tudor Cott)	II	15th or 16th century
The Crown	II	15th century

Lych Gate	II	15th century
St. Michael's Cottage	II	15th century
Oldfield View (formerly 1 & 3 Oldfield View)	II	17th & 18th century
Lych Gate Cottage	II	16th, 17th and 18th century
Yew Tree	II	G.V.
No. 3 Lych Gate	II	(Group Value)
Cottage to Hinds Head		
Hinds Head Hotel	II	15th century front 18th century
Nos. 1 & 2 (Cosy Cottages) Formerly 1 to 3 (consec) Cosy Cottages	II	17th & 18th century
Nos. 1 to 3 (consec) Lych Cottages	II	17th and 18th century

LISTED BUILDINGS– *additional notes.*

The Old Dutch House – "Late addition on left". Unspecified whether continuation of house, garden house, or garage-cum-staff-flat.

Chauntry Chapel of . . . "(converted later to Masters House). Also called The Old Schoolroom and now St Michael's Hall."

Chauntry House – "converted into flats." "Good staircase with carved string brackets. Panelled rooms."

The Crown – "one wing later addition."

Oldfield View – "Much altered and once two dwellings."

Lych Gate Cottage – The only single-storey in this group.

Hinds Head Hotel – "15th century with many alterations. Front new brick 18th century."

Nos. 1–2 Cosy Cottages – "continuous tiled roof abutting on public house."

Nos. 1 to 3 (consec) Lych Cottages – between Lych Gate and The Ringers. Continuous tiled roof abutting on public house.

THE CUT

At the time of the Inclosure Award, 1817–19, it was referred to as "Public Drain No. 1." Its course ran from Braywick roundabout eastwards across the fields to the river at Queens Eyot, where it still emerges today. Its origin is unknown, though there is a belief in some quarters that monks dug out the original channel.

It served to drain-off excess water from its surroundings for many years, but after several severe floods in the 19th and 20th centuries it was enlarged and re-routed to become the Maidenhead Relief Channel.

The work was undertaken by the Thames Conservancy, starting in 1960 at the river; reaching Hibbert Road, where the new bridge was built, in 1962; and finally reaching Maidenhead in 1967.

All Mod. Cons.

From J.W. Walker's "History of Maidenhead" we can elicit the following.

Mains Water. The Maidenhead Waterworks Company was formed in 1875 to supply Maidenhead, Bray and Cookham. Water was first supplied in 1876.

Gas. A company was formed in Maidenhead in 1835. As the then Vicar of Bray, the Rev. Walter Levett, was on the Management Committee, one imagines that he looked after the welfare of his parishioners and saw to it that Bray got its supply! In 1971 the old form of gas was discontinued in favour of North Sea Gas which was supplied in its place.

Electric Lighting. Current was formally switched-on in Maidenhead in December 1902, but Bray had to wait until August 1904 for its supply.

The first to enjoy it here were Jones' shop and the Hinds Head, but in times of floods they had to revert to large brass lamps. This trouble was eventually cured by laying an alternative cable along Braywick Road and Windsor Road, and thence via Upper Bray Road to the village.

Drainage. This was by cesspits, which were emptied by Cookham R.D.C.'s tankers until 1960, when main-drainage began. It was not compulsory to each householder immediately, but by 1962 the whole area had been connected.

Road-Sweeping used to be only a part of the whole job which included hedging and ditching beside the roads; also, before tarmac surfaces were applied the holes had to be mended with broken stone and flints which were tamped-in. Piles of the materials were kept on "Oldfield." i.e. Bray Green. Today the roads are the responsibility of the County Council (except for Hibbert Road which was taken over in 1934 by Maidenhead), and Bray is fortunate in having the services of Mr. Clinch who makes his rounds with his tools and yellow box-like trolley, wearing a regulation coloured jacket (to be more readily seen by motorists) and taking a great pride in his work of clearing up litter, sweeping up leaves, and keeping grass verges neat.

Litter-Bins on Bray Green, outside the Village Hall and by the War Memorial are cleared by Cookham R.D.C.

Telephone Kiosk. There is only one, standing at the junction of Brayfield Road and Old Mill Lane.

Post-Boxes. One is a circular pillar-box outside Jones' shop. The other, a small rectangular box attached to a wooden post (which will soon need renewing!) is in Old Mill Lane near the turning into River Gardens. Both are of EIIR vintage. There are two collections each day by van from both boxes and from the Post Office in the High Street at Morrells Shop (in earlier years "Thames House"). Deliveries to each house are also twice daily – one before breakfast and the next, mid-day.

In the early 1900's a carrier's cart brought the post from Maidenhead, handing over a heavy sack to a Mr. Crocker, an elderly man who nevertheless carried it on his back all round Holyport and Bray.

Later Mr. Stanley went the rounds on a bicycle. At Monkey Island it was necessary to ring the bell for the ferryman to come and collect the packages, right up to 1956 when the bridge was built over the backwater.

From 1904 Bray had its own post-mark for franking letters until about 1920.

Telegraph and Telephones. The first form of rapid communications was by telegraph from Maidenhead. One pair of wires went on poles down the Causeway, across to a pole in the High Street at the corner where the Hinds Head Coffee House now stands; and finally to Jones' shop where the messages were sent and received by morse-tapper. They had then to be written out and delivered by hand, whatever the weather and no matter how far away.

Telephones were not in use until 1907, the first subscribers being the Hinds Head and Jones. Our Mr. Harding, of Hope Cottage, helped to install these and subsequent lines.

Fire services, ambulance and police are all supplied from Maidenhead.

Library. Berkshire County Council has supplied this service since about 1950. The books were in a small room in the Village Hall, open once a week, until 1971. A local resident then gave the same service from her house for a year. Today it is in a Berkshire County Council caravan, calling at the village once a week.

"The un-named road," a short stretch between Ferry Road and Old Mill Lane, is now officially designated Brayfield Road. During Mr. Digby's years of property-development he separated "The Old Dutch House" from "Hillhouse Farm" at this point, making easier access to his building. It was closed once a year on Good Fridays to retain the property-rights but when he left it became a public road. From this crossing to the Albion, down Old Mill Lane, the road was likewise closed annually.

Perhaps this is the chapter in which to mention the *Bray Preservation Society*.

Early in 1965 "The Maidenhead Advertiser" publicized plans for gravel-extraction at Barge Farm, Taplow. Some 300 acres were to be worked during the coming 100 years. The proposed area, on the land opposite Bray, would have been a visible and audible horror which none could contemplate with any forbearance, let alone pleasure. Bray already had an example of it in Monkey Island Lane.

A meeting was called in St. Michael's Hall to register a protest and to set up an organisation to watch over the interests of the village. Mr. Geoffrey Coombes, of the Fisheries, presided, explained the position, and received solid support from a packed hall for the formation of the Bray Preservation Society. Officers and a committee were elected at once and Bray's bulldog was born. (Friendly beasts, bulldogs – unless their territory is threatened. Then they get their teeth in and hold on – and on – and on!)

As Chairman for the first six years I can speak from personal memory of the problems we became aware of, and tried to resolve. They ranged from would-be gravel operators and speculative builders to stretches of pavement and litter-bins. Other amenity societies sought our support in their battles and we returned the compliment. Our Council representatives at all three levels co-operated and ceased to be "the faceless ones" who could be neither approached nor persuaded of the needs of the population. By joining and regularly attending meetings of the River Thames Society and the Thames Planning Forum we tapped a further source of support on a wider and more forward looking scale. Here I would like to record and pay tribute to the tremendous amount of work done by Mr. Stanley Barrett, of Braybank, as secretary for four years. His tireless efforts to increase and then maintain a large membership bore fruit on more than one occasion at public enquiries where it became obvious that Bray spoke not only with their voices but with their pockets, and therefore must be listened to.

The present Committee, under the Chairmanship of

Captain Lloyd-Davies, has produced the "Bray Village Plan" – a document aiming at a constructive approach to the future of the village.

Problems have changed but little over the years. The original threats to the open fields and the threats to life and limb by the heavy traffic, remain.

With the imminent re-organisation of local government into large impersonal areas, such bodies as local Parish Councils and Amenity Societies are going to be vital for the welfare of ordinary citizens.

There will yet be times when we have to hold on – and on – and on.

PART SIX

HOME FROM SCHOOL

The following is an imaginary account of the return from school of pupils at any time between 1906–1914. The children's names are altered and dates have been telescoped; but places, objects, and occupations are genuine, also the anecdotes. It may give an idea of a part of the village life in those years.

With desks cleared, backs straight, and restless hands tightly clenched, it was the calm before the storm of happy irruption into the lanes.

The mistress stood in her neat white apron, smiling but inexorable, until the bell should ring. In the quietness could be heard the croaking of the frogs in Tad-Poole, the big pond behind the schoolhouse, and the screech of the peacocks on the lawn of Braywick Lodge. Mary and Meg were attuned to all things animal and vegetable, but while they heard these sounds, they were as ready as the rest to rush off immediately permission was given. It was a fine afternoon, and there were other things to see and hear on the way home.

As usual Meg had done her work well but with less effort than it had cost Mary who always had to concentrate harder, chew more pencils and use far more india-rubber to achieve her results. To both it was all tremendously interesting, but Meg had more energy left at the end of the day, and her natural tom-boy nature was ready for some physical action. Since they sat at the back of the class they had to control their excitement in the, perforce, orderly line of home-goers.

"Good-day, Meg."

"Good-day, Miss."

"Good-day, Mary."

"Good-day, Miss."

The last acknowledgement of both teacher and pupil of the day's mutual communication.

Then a clatter of feet, a babel of voices, and a general stampede to the school gate.

In their chosen groups, or singly, they went their ways.

George and his friends turned uphill; they were Braywick boys. They usually kicked up stones along the road or chased each other but today they were all concentrated upon one thing – the quickest way to the shop at the corner of the main road. George was jangling coins in his pocket, coins he had been given for helping the under-gardener at Canon Hill House, coins which enabled him to give free rein to his natural generosity. In excited anticipation they kept close together today.

At the top of the road stood Baker Allen's shop. The half-door opened easily, the small metal cow-bell announcing their arrival. There was always a variety of smells as they entered. Fresh bread and buns, hams hanging over their heads, bins and pencils, sawdust underfoot. Had they been with their parents they would have looked around at the variety of goods for sale but today was different. They went straight to the jars of sweets, arguing which was the best value. On one point all agreed. Something you could suck lasted longer. But their tastes differed. George's mathematics were not up to the task of dividing two halfpennies fairly between three people, but Mrs. Allen said it would be all right so the coins were handed over and, wonder of wonders, each boy was given his own small bag of sweets.

George felt so pleased that he actually remembered to say goodbye to Mrs. Allen before running after his two friends who already had a bulging cheek a-piece. Just in time he remembered he had to fetch a bundle from the washer-woman round the corner. He sucked hard on his bulls-eye and turned back.

She already had a hand cart packed with other deliveries for the district and was ready to start her rounds, but she told George where to find his, and he ran into the house.

Meg and Mary chose to return to Bray by the Causeway. On her way to school up Hibbert Rd, Meg had seen a horse and cart slewed into the ditch, the driver laying-on his whip in an attempt to make the horse get back onto the road. It had upset her a lot, and she didn't want to be reminded of the incident. Anyway, the Causeway held possibilities of search and discovery. There were trees with branches she could swing on if she really jumped for them. There might be a bird's nest she hadn't yet found. With the floods only a chilly memory the fields each side would be full of flowers in their various seasons, buttercups, king cups, water irises and Queen Anne's lace.

Mary agreed. She wouldn't be swinging on any branches or leaping over the ditches, but she enjoyed everything else the Causeway offered. There might be butterflies or even a Kingfisher if Meg could be persuaded to keep quiet at the Cut. But it was a vain hope – Meg whooped and jumped over the stream and on to the next bridge which crossed the damp ditch, with a deep hole beside the bridge.

"OOO," she shuddered, "Noakes Hole." It always fascinated her, this deep pool where legend had it that Noakes had drowned. Nobody could tell her when it had happened but her vivid imagination always painted horrific pictures of the drunken Noakes and his donkey falling here.

"No," replied Mary, "I don't want to hear it all again. Come on, lets go home. Just look at your muddy shoes and skirt. You'll catch it! Tell you what, I'll race you to the end."

She knew she wouldn't win, but it was a "dare" that would bring Meg leaping back – and it did.

When they reached Oldfield the road mender was preparing to leave. A good pile of stones and flints bore witness to his afternoon's work. He had to keep the roadside hedges and ditches in good shape as well as the road surface, filling-in holes caused by flooding or by traffic. Chipping the stones was hard work but he took a pride in it and was well-liked in the village.

Meg's burst of wildness was over. She made some attempt to smooth her hair, and wiped her shoes on the grass before walking through the village. At Holmans Mat (or what was left of it) the two girls parted company, Mary going down the new road towards the Ferry. At Hillhouse Farm she was puzzled by a noise she couldn't identify. Pulling herself up the wall she looked over. There in the byre was a cow giving birth to a calf. Wide-eyed, she waited until the little creature wobbled uncertainly on its thin legs. Then, bursting with the need to tell someone about it, she ran home as fast as she could. No clambering over the heaps of coal by the wharf today. She *must* tell her mother about the calf.

Meanwhile, others had taken the Hibbert Road route. Some of the boys made straight for the river-crossing at Hogge Bridge, and going down Church Road, they could get quickly to the river bank, take off their boots, roll up their sleeves and lie looking into the water for whatever swam or floated their way. You never knew what flotsam and jetsam might arrive – there was always a hope.

More slowly came three girls, chatting of this and that, and keeping close together as they approached the field on the corner. Eva and Alice were always afraid that Harry Pilcher might speak to them, but Emily was never frightened by him. "My Dad says he's only barmy and won't hurt anyone" she repeated time and again, but the others didn't believe her. "He was so odd. He lived in a hut in the corner of the field and wouldn't let anyone go near it, he had a terrible temper, and . . ."

But Emily knew more about him and would tell anyone who asked, "It's quite sad, really. Poor Harry Pilcher! He was a naval officer who had some clever invention which was stolen from him. He was so upset that it turned his brain and he was put in a mental home. But he couldn't stand being shut up and broke out from wherever he was, so it was thought better to let him be in the open. He's quite handsome, really. So tall and broad, and neat in his plus-fours. And with his moustache and small beard he looks like Drake.

Inside his hut he sleeps on a pile of drainpipes, and my Dad gave him some horse-blankets as covers. Somebody said they'd seen him one night riding on his cow, facing its tail, and going round and round the field in the moonlight shouting "Harry! Harry! Harry!" But he's got a goat now and milks that. He takes it on a lead into the village. It's funny watching him go to Jones' shop. He does all sorts of antics on the way, and when he gets there he turns on his heels, clicks them smartly, and marches into the shop. They give him cheese and fruit.

He sometimes comes into our kitchen for a warm by the fire and a hot drink. He's quiet then, but if he gets wild Dad can calm him. One day in Maidenhead, Dad found him holding a coloured man by the nape of the neck and the seat of his pants and rubbing him up and down the road. The onlookers were laughing at him, and that made him more angry than ever and he wouldn't stop. But Dad was able to calm him and he let go of the man and came home in our cart."

But we've digressed.

Eva and Alice were with Emily on the way home, down Hibbert Road. When they reached the cross-roads they met the cattle being driven from Gaskins Mead to their milking-shed – not far away, just down the lane opposite the Church Drive.

Emily's father was leaning on the wall of Chauntry House, where he and his wife were looking after the house for Mr. Leslie Lloyd Bailey while he was away. With him was the drover who came each year, driving his sheep from Scotland to Hyde Park for the sheep-dog trials. The cost of the journey was defrayed by the services of the sheep in cropping churchyards en route, and by hospitality to the shepherd. This was a regular annual occurrence in Bray. All exits from the church yard were closed while the sheep were there.

Emily joined the two men, and heard her Dad telling the shepherd about the runaway stag.

"Last Christmas Eve it came racing through the village and up this drive. I tried to catch it but it careered around faster than I could move. Eventually it rushed across the road into the kitchen-garden opposite. That's the gardener's cottage over there, and he went after it till it was driven against the fence at the end. Between us we got it back to the stables here and shut it in. Later on, a huntsman arrived. He said it would have to stay here over Christmas and he brought a van on Boxing Day to take it away. But the gardener – phew! – he was angry at the way his vegetables had been trampled!"

When she got into the house she found the gypsy woman sitting by the fire smoking her clay pipe. What with the baccy and her dirty clothes she smelt horrible, but Mr. Lloyd Bailey had given orders that whenever she came she was to be given food, warmth and money. According to him, she had been born in a ditch in Norfolk, where his family lived, and she wandered south and back each year. That was all they knew about her.

Seeing the child's nose wrinkle in disgust Emily's mother tactfully suggested she could fetch the shoes from the cobbler's.

As she ran thankfully to the gate there was a clatter from the opposite corner. Two boys had been playing among the pile of bricks and junk in what had once been a garden shed. It was a popular pastime with the young and caused no comment. At the coach house beside it Mr. Norsworthy was returning the trap he had re-painted.

She waved to him and went on.

In front of the Hinds Head some boys were pretending to

be the German band which had played there last week. A drum and a penny-whistle were hardly representative of the genuine article, but imagination filled the gaps. On a Sunday morning the scene was very different. The gentry arrived in their carriages which would then be driven here, the horses taken from the shafts and stabled behind the inn until it was time to reassemble the equipage for the homeward journey. In these days the church services were much longer; sermons tended to be a trial of strength both for the vicar and his congregation; and the full service of The Book of Common Prayer was rigidly adhered to – small wonder, then, that while their masters were attending to the refreshment of their souls, their coachmen should take some refreshment in the inn.

Eva was standing with a basket outside Blackall's cottage, next to the Ringers Inn, watching him at his "snobbing." It was always fascinating to see him with a cheekful of tacks, spitting one out as he needed it for repairing the shoes.

"Granny Blackall", as the children called her, was leaving with a sack over her shoulder containing repaired shoes and boots to be delivered, some as far away as Windsor Rd. She had nine children to support, and it meant long hours of work to provide for them all. There were two other families of similar size in the village, all of them kept spotlessly clean and rosy-cheeked – no small feat in those days of low wages.

Eva and Emily stood together a while, silent.

"D'you suppose he ever swallows one?"

"Don't know. But I'm glad I don't have to do it. Oh well I'd better see if Mother's shoes are ready."

"Yes – and I suppose I'd better take this laundry from Granny Whalley round to Ferry End. See you tomorrow morning when the bell rings."

The bell was a large and loud bell above Miss Roquetts house. It was rung punctually at 8.30 every weekday and had become the recognised signal to the children that it was time they left for school.

Granny Whalley lived at "The Limes," beside the Lych-gate. It was a Georgian house where she had the curate to live, and did the laundry for several people. Her drying ground was her garden behind the house. Hers was a busy life and she was glad to pay a few pennies to any children who offered to deliver the washing.

When Eva went round to Ferry End she saw Ted talking to a friend.

"Looks different, doesn't it? The road's wider, and you couldn't have another fair, with its stalls, on this piece of grass, could you? Holmans Mat has gone for good. Remember the big orchard there used to be where these houses are? They could fetch £400 each, but they're let now. I talked to the men building them. The labourers got paid 4d an hour, and the foreman 6d."

Eva opened the gate. £400! Fancy having so much money to spend! She clutched her penny more tightly.

Her errand completed, she returned home to the old cottage in Church Lane in time to see her father going out.

"Where are you going? Can I come with you?"

"Yes, of course. I'm just going to feed the vicar's pony."

They crossed the churchyard and went out through the kissing-gate on the opposite corner. The stables were just across the Vicarage drive.

Meanwhile Ted had gone to the bicycle shop by "The Crown." His bike had suffered yet another puncture, and he just hoped it had been mended again – new tyres had to be earned or saved-up for. There were too many stones and flints in Bray streets for his liking. Dusty they were, too. When the carriages and coaches came through in Ascot week great clouds of dust covered anyone near them. In the High St. it was as well to keep your windows shut that week, unless you wanted extra cleaning.

As he emerged with his bike there was a crash.

From nowhere and everywhere a crowd gathered. Mr. Digby had backed his new motorcar known locally as

"Digby's hearse," into one of the hitching posts outside Baker Mark's shop.

Not surprisingly the air was becoming thick with expletives. His was the first car in Bray and as with all "progress" there were those who considered it noisy, smelly, and unnecessary. This episode only strengthened their opinion and elicited little sympathy.

Not so Ted. He had a lively interest in cars, which he was to retain all his life.

However there was nothing he could do to help, so with a "Bad luck, sir," and a friendly smile he turned back.

On his way home he went into Jones's shop. His bike repair hadn't cost too much and he had a penny or two to spare for some sweets. With any luck Mr. Tom would serve him. He had a soft spot for children and would fill a cone of paper from the tilted jar till it was full to the top. If you only had a halfpenny it was just the same to him. Maybe it was the loss of profits in this department, which forced Mrs. Jones to be more meticulous in her weighing of other goods. Business is business, after all.

By the time he emerged from the shop the car had coughed and hiccupped away and the street had emptied. It was time for the evening meal, and he cycled past Sealey's shop to his home.

SCHOOLS

In 1683 William Cherry, Squire of Shottesbrook, provided the first school in the parish. He converted the old Chauntry Chapel, behind the church, into a schoolroom and library, and installed a master to whom he paid £20 per annum for teaching "twenty poor boys of the Parish."

The scholars were drawn from a wide area, probably some from "Maidenhead in Bray" and certainly one from White Waltham. This was Thomas Hearne who was to become the celebrated antiquary. He walked the three miles from White Waltham Vicarage to Bray, night and morning; to be taught "the rudiments of the Latin tongue, some time about 1693" (Kerry).

In 1799, the records show the school being run by Trustees who had the right to nominate one boy each, while the chairman and treasurer (i.e. the Vicar) could nominate two.

In that year the master's duties were: to teach twenty boys reading, writing, accounts and the Church catechism; to make no demand whatever upon the free scholars otherwise than for pens, ink, books, and fire; "at his own expence (*sic*) keep all the windows and the pump in good repair"; and to take the scholars to church every Sunday.

The school hours were from 7 o'clock till 12 from April 15th to October 15th, with an hour for breakfast from 9–10 a.m. During the rest of the year from 9 to 12 o'clock with no time off for breakfast, and in the afternoon from 1–5 o'clock from April 15th to October 15th, and from 1–4 o'clock during the remainder of the year.

"The Holidays shall be for one calendar month beginning on the Monday before Christmas Day, for two weeks in the Hay Harvest and the same time at the Corn Harvest."

"Every Saturday shall be an half Holiday, the boys being kept until 1 o'clock to repeat the Church catechism." The only other holidays were Good Friday, Easter Eve, and Easter week; Whit Monday and Tuesday and Holy Thursday; Ash Wednesday; and the King's and Queen's birthdays.

Boys could be expelled for non-attendance or for non-payment for pens etc.

The harvest holidays were given to enable the children to help in the fields, a wise move since they were unlikely to turn up at school when everybody else was enjoying themselves in the open air! In that year the age-range was only from 8–12 years, and they would probably have been some help in the field-work too.

By the 19th century numbers had grown beyond the capacity of the Chauntry Chapel, with all except the "20 poor boys" paying from 2–4s a week for their education, according to their fathers' financial capabilities. Some other accommodation had to be found, and the Trustees arranged with Mr. Pascoe Grenfell to lease, for one year, the old Manor Court.

This was the building in Hibbert Road which had, for centuries, been the Court House "containing two rooms, with a parcell of land there unto adjoining, containing by estimation one acre and a half, valued per ann. at thirty-three shillings, four pence." Part of "the parcell" was the Pound, where stray animals were kept until redeemed by their owners.

The Court dealt with all manner of complaints, quarrels, and legal disputes. Kerry quotes (from the Bray Court Rolls) that in 1517 an Alice Smythgate of Braywick" is a babbler (garulatrix) and has an unruly tongue; wherefore the said Alice is commanded to refrain herself . . . under penalty of 40s and bodily punishment," the latter probably implying the stocks or whipping-post at Touchen End. One imagines that such severe threats put an end to her slanderous gossiping, for her husband would have found the fine too much on his small wages, and taken steps to control the situation!

By 1819 the whole system was changing, Maidenhead was taking a greater, if sometimes muddled, part in local affairs, and the Manor Court was no longer needed.

The new school retained the "20 poor boys," though they are now recorded as "20 poor children" so one may surmise that girls were also eligible by then. The terms of reference alter too. Instruction is to be in "reading, writing and arithmetic, and morality and religion according to the doctrines of the Church of England." The age-range is extended to "from 6 to 14 years of age. School attendances are to be recorded by the schoolmaster and vouched for by the Vicar," as the master's salary is linked to the number of pupils during the whole or part of a year. He received 16s per head per annum.

The daily records show a good deal of truancy, and failure to pay the agreed pennies. This often leads to expulsion in favour of others waiting for the chance of even so limited a form of education.

Some twenty-eight years later a further expansion is needed. Land in Holyport is given by the Fishmonger's Company and all boys of 8 years and over are sent there. Braywick thereupon becomes a school for girls up to 14 years, plus small boys.

A charity is formed for supplying needy children with black boots, round black hats with a red hat-band, and a length of cloth to make a dress or a coat. Until about 1939 the goods were provided by Moore's of Maidenhead, who arrived every year with large sacks of the clothing and fitted-out each child eligible for it. Latterly the allocation dwindled, and a few parents received vouchers which they took to the shop in the High Street. The remainder of the money was then laid out to bread and meat until 1939, when coals were substituted, and today it takes the form of groceries each Christmas, provided via Jones' shop in Bray.

The Old Schoolroom had reverted to church and parish uses and in 1901 was "opened three evenings per week as a Reading Room" by the Vicar, the Reverend C. A. Raymond.

With increasing Government control and contributions to general education Braywick became a "primary" school, and so remained until this year (1973). It has now moved to the new building behind the housing estate on Bray Road, and is called "Oldfield School." The Hibbert Road site is occupied by Winbury School, from Maidenhead.

PART SEVEN

UP-TO-DATE

And up-to what? How do we fill our days? It depends, of course, on how old or young we are.

If we were born here during Victoria or Edward VII's reign we will probably live in a cottage, or Jesus Hospital, or Hanover Mead. Very few are in larger dwellings. We would not lack friends and neighbours and others to keep an eye on our welfare. We might go to the Darby and Joan Club in Holyport twice a month; the Women's Institute at Bray Village Hall once a month; to Matins on Sundays and Holy Communion on Wednesday mornings; to the Mothers' Union. Once a week we would collect our Old Age Pension from the post office (£7.75 single, £12.50 married couple); shopping in Maidenhead would be either by car or by bus, but we would tend to make essential purchases at Jones' or Bowler's. The National Bus Company runs a service of 14 buses per day into Maidenhead and back.

For those who need it, there is a scheme of meals-on-wheels which is provided by the Womens Royal Voluntary Service in Maidenhead. A hot two-course meal is delivered twice each week; chiropody is also a free service.

There are several of this generation in Bray today and much of what is printed here is due to their kindness and patience in answering innummerable questions over the past twelve months. It has been astonishing to find their memories so seldom disagreeing, rather have they unwittingly supplemented each others' accounts.

The next age-group – let us say roughly from sixty to forty – are probably still busy bringing-home-the-bacon. The vast majority of the men commute to work in London,

Slough, Windsor, Reading or Maidenhead. In many cases both parents go out to work. As the children are at school all day and modern household appliances make the chores simpler, many women prefer to return to some paid occupation which also provides the companionship of fellow-workers. Others may work with voluntary organisations in the nearby towns – others again, find their homes and families fill their days sufficiently. Probably 95% of the men of all ages below retirement are away from the village all day.

Leisure activities for this group tend to be mainly of an evening. The only exclusively male ones are the British Legion; the Church of England Mens' Society; and billiards in the Village Hall Club (though this is male-dominated by custom rather than decree). For most men the routine is off to work between eight and eight-thirty, by car, or by train from Maidenhead. Home again between 6 and 7.30 p.m. Relax, eat, and settle down to the evening's occupations – many to watch or fall asleep in front of "the telly"!

Some, both male and female, take part in local activities, acting on committees of various kinds (e.g. Village Hall, Bray Preservation Society, Parish Council, Parochial Church Council). As in most communities the number of people both able *and* willing to serve is relatively small, and the same names tend to be found on more than one committee. Not so long ago these would have been mostly from the over-forties, but today many younger people are doing their share.

The life-style of this younger group is similar to the previous one except that the young mums do not take on day-time activities outside their homes until the youngest child is able to go to pre-school play-group in the Village Hall in the mornings, and evenings-out have to be catered for by importing a baby-sitter for the requisite hours, unless one is fortunate enough to have a resident "au pair girl," a modern "invention" which fills some of the gaps left by the nannies and domestic staff of yesteryear. It has been noticeable over the past twelve years that more prams and junior cyclists and budding horse-women are met around the village. In 1958 the number of children under ten could be counted on one hand.

The children go to various schools here and in Maidenhead, and are mostly transported by car. Not for them the three-mile tramp each end of the day which Hearne, the antiquary, found worthwhile in the 17th century! There are primary schools at Holyport and Oldfield, the latter opened this year in place of the Braywick School in Hibbert Road which has now been taken over by Winbury School from Maidenhead. A private boys' preparatory school, its playing fields border Hibbert Road on the Maidenhead side.

There is a Girl Guide Company and a Brownie pack in Bray every week in the Village Hall. Scouts and Cub /Scouts have to go to Holyport. The senior branches of the movement are short on numbers due to the ever-increasing pressure of homework for teenagers working for their 'O' level and 'A' level examinations.

Hockey and cricket at the Sports Club are available for the male students, and riding is becoming increasingly popular. Sailing on Bray reach is a non-starter. A few try it from time to time but eventually admit defeat and transfer to Cookham or Bourne End. Rowing is organised from the Maidenhead Rowing Club.

For all there is the normal va-et-vient of entertaining in the homes, but the large and hilarious parties in the large houses have disappeared with the elimination or subdivision of such houses. Perhaps one feature of this age, not known before, is the coffee-morning. This may be a private affair between friends or in aid of some good cause needing funds, in which case it usually includes a bring-and-buy stall and a raffle.

Perhaps the gayest of Bray's evenings recently were at the Village Hall on April 3 and 4 1970. These were "Edwardian Evenings" when all wore the dress of the period and enjoyed the old-fashioned Music Hall entertainment organised by Mrs. Jennifer Gough. The hall was packed to capacity with the old and the young, singing and laughing together. Surely the ghosts of times past must have floated around the Hall with amusement and pleasure that week!

A cheese-and-wine party combined with a display of work by local artists is an annual event which is popular. And this Autumn we propose to have a "Bray Day" when objects old and new concerning Bray, and the originals of the illustrations in this book, will be on display. Tea in the afternoon and a cheese-and-wine party in the evening will allow most of the local inhabitants to take part.

Life today is very different from that of "the Furest" and the "bogges." The largely agricultural occupations ceased with the building developments on Hill House Farm and the Mill estate by Mr. T.J. Digby and his followers, but there are still the open fields of Weir Bank Farm and the fields to the west of the High Street. These preserve the village atmosphere which is so greatly valued by us all. Long may they remain, for

"THIS IS OUR VILLAGE."

PART EIGHT

BRITISH PLACE NAMES

Mr. Michael H.H. Bayley, A.R.I.B.A. Dipl. Arch. Oxford has very kindly given permission for the inclusion here of some of his theories and findings as to the Cornish, Welsh, or British origins of some names in Bray, Braywick, and near by.

Sawkins Bridge – YSA KENS BRIVA – The lowest former pre-Roman bridge.

Garston's Mead – GARAN-ES-TOWAN – The Cranes gravel-ridge island.

Hog Bridge – EOG BRIVA – Salmon Bridge.

Charlese – CHARN-LAIS – The stones of the clear water.

Easthay Field – GAEAF-HAY – The winter enclosed pasture.

Bedemede – BEDD MAES DN – The tomb of the open cattle-field.

Canon Hill – CAE-NANT HEOL – the enclosed field by the stream of the road.

Headpile (Eyot) – ENEDGE PIL – The fast creek.

Braywick – BRIVA GWK – The bridge creek.

Braywick – BRIVA-VICUS – The Roman villa of the bridge.

Wykemead – WYKEMEDE (in 1489) – Braywick Mead.

Builders Cross – BEILI DUWIES CROES – The courtyard of the goddess of the tumulus (of death?).

Builders Well – BEILI DUWIES WY LLE – The water-place of the goddess of the courtyard of the mound.

Monkey Island – MON CAE YS LLAN – The sacred enclosure of the cow (goddess) of the cornfield.

Queen's Eyot – QUIDDEN EBYR TIR – The Holy Land of tumulus of the confluence of rivers.

Down Place – TOWAN PLAS – The mansion of the gravel bank.

Water Oakley – WARTHA EOG LLE – The upper Salmon Place.

Harvest Hill – HAVOS HIEL – The road to the summer shielings.

Kimbers Lane – CYMER-BURGRIL – Shepherds junction.

In the church is a SHELA-NA-GIG. This is an ancient fertility symbol sometimes to be seen on the outside of buildings, but in Bray's Church it is inside on the pillar at the left-hand side of the west door. Though beheaded it is recognisable by students of the period. So, too, is the carved stone in the wall of St. Michael's Hall which portrays Hecate's messenger, the dog.

PART NINE

BRAY INCLOSURE AWARD

For those who are unfamiliar with the Inclosure Awards the following explanatory notes provided by the Berkshire Record Office may be of interest.

The term 'inclosure award' is usually applied to the document which concludes the process of inclosure of common lands, open fields and waste lands by Act of Parliament in the eighteenth and nineteenth centuries. But the diminution of open field lands from various causes is a phenomenon that had begun in Middle Ages.

By the early sixteenth century the conversion of arable land to pasture had become a subject of public anxiety, especially when it involved depopulation of villages. The findings of commissioners appointed to inquire into it in Berkshire and other counties in 1517 have been published in *The Domesday of Inclosures* (1897). Hostility declined, however, and from the end of the sixteenth century inclosures by agreement between the lord of the manor and his tenants are found. In places in north west Berkshire in the sixteenth and seventeenth centuries, several cases are known of such agreements being forrmally confirmed by a decree of the Court of Chancery. Agreements to inclose were also sometimes confirmed by private Acts of Parliament as at Aston Tirrold, 1742–3.

When the procedure of inclosure began to be regulated in advance by Act of Parliament, this could take several different forms. According to an Act of 1756, (29 Geo. II c. 36), inclosures were permitted by agreement between lords of manors and tenants for the purpose of planting and preserving timber. But inclosures made in this way relate only to small areas of land in a few Forest parishes such as Old

Windsor. Special local Acts were secured in advance by some parishes for a more general inclosure to be carried out by one or more commissioners. But, as this was found very expensive, procedure was later simplified by the passing of a series of General Inclosure Acts, notably in 1801 (41 Geo. III c. 109), 1836, (6 & 7 Wm. IV c.115), 1845 (8 & 9 Vict. c. 118), and 1876 (39 & 40 Vict. c. 56). These Acts contained detailed provisions for deciding practical and financial aspects of the matter, such as the powers of the inclosure commissioners, payment of compensation, ownership of land, and sales and exchange of land. Acts of Parliament were then obtained for particular places to complete the detail of the procedure according to local circumstances. It is quite possible for there to be more than one award, by more than one procedure, for different areas in the same parish.

The formal documents eventually produced consist of the award, either on the pattern of a large deed (i.e. several large sheets of parchment fastened at the lower edge), or a volume or a continuous roll, with an accompanying map or map attached. The opening passages of an award usually mention the lands to be inclosed, the Act or Acts under which inclosure was made, the meetings held by the commissioners and the appointment of a surveyor of the lands. They then go on to define public and private roads and footpaths, these usually being numbered in some way. Allotments of lands to the lord of the manor, incumbent of the church and other landowners usually follow, the number and acreage of the land given in the margin corresponding with the same particulars on the map.

Most maps illustrate the field system after the inclosure had taken place and do not therefore show strips in the fields. (But these may be shown on the commissioners' working plans where they survive.) The maps can only be used to a limited extent as a guide to the ownership of land or houses. Nevertheless some do show in detail the outline of the houses in the village and may mark other prominent topographical features such as brick kiln, paper mill, tumulus or wharf.

BRAY INCLOSURE AWARD 1817–1819

The following notes refer to extracts from the documents and map of the area covered by this book. They are taken from the two copies, respectively at Berkshire County Archives and the Oxford Diocesan Records. (It may be of use here to note that the two records differ very slightly, but possibly significantly in any legal argument. See under "General Allotments, No. 92".)

In the map, the darker shaded portions refer to pasture land; the lighter is arable; while in the original map the whole of the built-up area of the village between Gaskin's Mead and Old Mill Lane is left white. So, too, are the riverside properties of "Geo. White" and "Richard Webb" and land marked with personal names. The old wharf area is noted as belonging to "K. Woodhouse."

First, then, the roads. These are "Publick" and "Private."

Publick Road No. 1.	the Windsor Road
Publick Road No. 2.	Upper Bray Road
Publick Road No. 10	Hibbert Road and High Street
Private Road No. 31	Monkey Island Lane and Old Mill
Private Road No. 32	no longer exists. It led from 31 to R. Webb's land.
Private Road No. 33	is roughly the line of the lane leading from 31 to Monkey Island

Publick Drain No. 1 is described as "15 ft. wide commencing at Braywick and running through Braymead into the Thames near Monkey Island;" marked on the map merely as No. 1 it is known to us as The Cut, but in its former route.

General Allotments

It is impossible to quote every one in full but here are some examples.

No. 71 a. r. p. 3 1 20

Unto the Wardens and Commonalty of the Mystery of Fishmongers of the City of London . . . in Wick Mead . . . bounded on the N by Inclosure of the said Wardens and Commonalty and of Basil Woodhouse, and on E by Publick Road No. 2, and on the S by Publick Drain No. 1. and on the W by an allotment to Joseph Slack.

No. 45 a. r. p. 12 3 23

Unto the Deans and Canons of the King's Free chapel of St. George within his Castle of Windsor . . . situate in Bray Field containing 12 acres 3 rods and 23 perches bounded on the N.E. by the River Thames, and on the E by an allotment to Patrick Cranfurd Bruce and the Private Road No. 33 on the S by the Private Road No. 31 and on the W by an allotment to Charles Augustus Hoare.

No. 92 a. r. p. 1 2 22

Bray Common Allotment. Bounded on N by Allotment to John Bowyer (now The Orchard) on W by Allotment to William Payne Esq. (now Lewis field) and the public footway (Causeway) and on NE by Publick Road No. 10 (Bray High St. by Sports Club) . . . to be used as Common of Pasture in the following proportions.

Proprietor	*Occupier*	*No. of Messuage*	*No. of Cattle*
Benbow Joseph	Richard Footman	1	1
Buckland Ann	John Lawrence	1	1
Butler Mary	Polly Wells	1	1
Finmore George	James Collins	1	1
Hawkins Thomas	Richard Lock & others	1	1
Jones William	Self	1	1
McQueen John Donald	Workhouse	1	1
Mason Martha	Timothy Webb	1	1

Nelsey (late Bennet)	Richard Beasley & others	1	1
Oxford (Bishop of)	George Homan	1	1
Pile James	Matthew Crutchfield	1	1
Stevens William	Self	1	1
Ward Thomas	Self	1	1
Wells Polly	William Chapman	1	1
White Mary	Self	1	1
Willis Mrs.	Solomon Wilkins	1	1
		Total 16	

(Fences on NE (i.e. High Street) maintained by above.)

No. 92 is one place where the two maps differ. There is in the Diocesan copy a further small area numbered 92 also of which it is said:

> "Unto John Donal McQueen M.D. . . . (being part of the Poor House Garden, given up in exchange by the Rev. Edward Townshend) containing 24 perches bounded on the E and S by Publick Roads and on the N and W by the other part of the said garden."

(1) The County copy calls it "Bray Garden. John Donald McQueen. 24 perches only."

(2) This is now part of the driveway from the main gate into Chauntry House.

Of Gaskins Mead (97) it is said:

> ". . . being an old inclosure received in exchange from the Bishop of Oxford . . . 6 acres, 27 perches . . . Bounded on the NW by the River Thames and old inclosures of Geo. White on the SE by the Church Yard and The Workhouse Garden and on the SW by Publick Road No. 10 on the W by other allotments to the said Vicar of Bray."

Gaskins is sometimes called Garstons (1677) but one old terrier of 1783 refers to it as "Gascoigne's, bounded by the Churchyard" which seems a reasonable predecessor to Gaskins.

Plots	*Name and Owners*	*1973*
97	Gaskins Mead Vicarial Tithe	Sports Club
93	John Bowyer	
94	Zechariah Boult as lessee of Bishop of Oxford	
92	Old Field Bray Common Allotment	Bray Green
Also 92 see above notes	Unto John Donal McQueen M.D. . . . (being part of the Poor House Garden, given up in exchange by the Rev. Edward Townshend containing 24 perches bounded on E and S by Publick Roads and on N and W by the other part of the said garden (fences by McQueen) Now – Driveway into Chauntry House, from main gate	
89	Old Field	Bray Broc
90	Rev. Edward Townshend	
91	Old Field William Payn Esq.	open field
90a	Bray Inclosure	Fields by Causeway
90b	Bishop of Oxford	
52	Bray Field Wm. Edward Woodhouse	Braybank flats
51	Bray Field John Lewis	Old Mill Lane, River Gardens and field between Old Mill Lane and M.4
48	Bray Field	
49	Chas. Augustus Hoare	Brayfield Road and Weirbank Farm
53	Bray Field Fishmonger's Co.	Hanover Mead and Allotments
54	Bray Field James Clark	
55	Bray Field Reading Corporation	Weirbank Farm cut by M.4
66	Holyport Field Charles Haye Esq.	Weirbank Farm cut by M.4
67	Holyport Field	Court House and M.4

	Thomas Groom	Weirbank Farm, Roes Field
68	Wick Mead Countess of Orkney	Weirbank Farm, Roes Field
69	Wick Mead Thomas Ward	
70	Wick Mead Pascoe Grenfell Esq.	Weirbank Farm
71	Wick Mead Fishmongers Co.	Fishmonger's
72	Wick Mead Joseph Albion Slack	Woodhouse
73	Wick Mead Emma Law	Lucas field
74	Holyport Field Richard Webb	Canon Hill Close and Hasting Close
85	Old Field Thomas Anbury	Bray Broc
81	Hibbert Rd Emma Law	Front gardens of cottages
86	Old Field Joseph Albion Slack	Halcyon Cottage
87	Old Field Geo. White	Red Eyot
83	Old Field Richard Webb	
82	Old Field Sir Jonathan Walker Waller	
88	Old Field Mary White	
84	Old Field Sir Jonathan Walker Waller	
50	Bray Field Mary White	South of Mill
48	Bray Field Chas. Augustus Hoare	Weir Bank or vegetable field
45	Bray Field *D and C's Windsor	Weir Bank

46	Bray Field John White	Monkey Island Hotel and Long White Cloud
47	Bray Field P. C. Bruce Esq.	Monkey Island Hotel car park
43	Bray Field D and C's Windsor	
42	Bray Field D and C's Windsor	
15	Water Oakley Field	
13	Jane Cooper	
35	Water Oakley Field John Dellar	Clericus, Pomona Farm, etc.
36	Water Oakley Field Thomas Groom	Pomona and Gravel Pit
37	Fifield Field John Westbrook	Gravel Pit and garage
40	Berry Pits Chas. Fuller	Gravel Pit and houses
38	Berry Pits Surveyor and Highways	
39	Berry Pits John Hercy	
41	Bray Field D and C's Windsor	Weirbank Farm
54	Bray Field James Clark	Weirbank Farm
44	Bray Field D and C's Windsor	

* Dean and Canons of St. George's Chapel, Windsor